THE ZENSATIONAL BUDDHA
THE BUDDHA, FROM A ZEN PERSPECTIVE

BY

RAHUL KARN

DEDICATED TO

THE BUDDHA
(THE ENLIGHTENED ONE)
&
MY WIFE JYOTI
(THE LIGHT)

PREFACE

Dear Zen Friends,

Hope you have not won a lottery recently! Well, fortunately, or unfortunately, people come to Buddha, not when there is some exciting event happening in their lives. People mostly come when they are going through some adversities. Trust me, you will find these stories very exciting and sometimes even shocking!
Unlike traditional Buddhists, Zen people have a very special relationship with Buddha. When you talk to a close friend, how do you call him? Do you call him by saying, "Your Majesty or His Highness friend"? No. You call him mate or dear. Similarly, these Zen people sometimes call Buddha with salutations, which looks rude superficially. But, deep down they love him. How can anyone hate a cool person like Buddha? Who can love Buddha more than a Zen master who devotes his whole life walking on the path of Buddha?
In this book, I have brought for you a collection of those Zen stories which mostly look weird or shocking. In some stories, the Zen Master will not bow in front of the Buddha statue, in some, the master might burn down the wooden Buddha statue and in some, the master may even allow others to spit on the Buddha! But this is not out of any kind of hatred. This is a special kind of love.
There might be various reasons behind such episodes:

i. The master performs the weird act out of friendly love towards Buddha.

ii. The master wants the student to be self-dependant. Buddha has himself said that just praying to Buddha will not help; rather one has to work hard on meditation himself.

iii. The master wants the student to realize that the truth is beyond words. The truth is a matter of experience. So, not get too much attached to words. Thus, some Zen masters have called the Buddha - a liar. Some Zen masters have said that the Buddha misguided humanity. These masters simply want to pontificate you to not get too much attached to Buddha or his words. Rather, dive deep into meditation.

iv. Zen Master Rinzai used to say: Kill the Buddha. He just wants to say that when you go deep in meditation, you might hear peaceful sounds or see peaceful forms. You might even see Buddha in your meditation. Don't stop there. Kill the Buddha and keep going. Don't get stuck on sound or forms. Keep progressing.

v. Finally, Zen says that there is nowhere to go. We are already in the truth because the truth always is and how can one be in something which isn't? So, there is no need to do anything including investigation about Buddha!

One more thing: Buddha word has been used in two broad senses:

I. The person Gautama, The Buddha
II. The quality of the Buddha, the enlightenment

With these insights, if you study these cases then I am sure you would have a totally different Zensational viewpoint of seeing the Buddha.

The present work is the outcome of my over 9 years of study and research of Zen classics. As you will see, these cases have been taken from over fifty sources. Sometimes, the same case is present in more than one classic. In the end, I have given the list of references from which these cases are taken. Curious readers can refer them if they want to do a further study of Zen classics. Some people prefer Chinese names of the Zen Masters whereas others prefer to call them with their Japanese names. I have used both conventions here.

Earlier, I had thought of writing explanatory commentaries on these cases. But then I thought, not to condition you with my vision and leave you alone with the Zensational Buddha!

I am sure after reading this book, you will be able to see the Buddha and understand his teachings from a totally different perspective than a traditional Buddhist. That understanding will not be anything less than winning a lottery!

Should you have any queries, please don't hesitate to contact me on zensationalstories@gmail.com.

Have a Zensational time!

Your Zen Friend,
Rahul Karn
Melbourne
5th of June 2019

Contents

- THE TRUE HOMAGE 1
- SHAKYAMUNI WAS AN ORDINARY OLD FELLOW 2
- THE LIAR BUDDHA 4
- THE MISGUIDER BUDDHA 5
- KILL THE BUDDHA 6
- BUDDHA: THE DRIED PIECE OF EXCREMENT 7
- TALK WITHIN A DREAM 9
- BLACK-NOSED BUDDHA 10
- THE TEACHING OF THE WHOLE LIFETIME 11
- THE LAST WILL AND TESTAMENT 12
- THE MOST IMPORTANT TEACHING 14
- ZEN TEACHINGS OF BODHIDHARMA 15
- NOTHING EXISTS 19
- A PHILOSOPHER ASKS BUDDHA 20
- BUDDHA TWIRLS A FLOWER 21
- THE MEANING 22
- NO TRANSMISSION 23
- DESHAN'S "ASSEMBLY ON VULTURE PEAK" 24
- THE WORLD-HONORED ONE ASCENDS THE TEACHING SEAT 25

A BUDDHA BEFORE HISTORY	26
TOZAN'S THREE POUNDS	27
DRIED DUNG	28
NOT MIND, NOT BUDDHA, NOT THINGS	29
MAZU'S "MIND IS BUDDHA"	30
YOU ARE ALREADY A BUDDHA	31
MAÑJUSRI ENTERS THE GATE	33
BAOFU'S BLOCKING OF THE EYES, EARS, AND MIND	34
JOSHU AND THE GREAT BUDDHA	35
WHO'S THE BUDDHA?	36
THE AIM	37
WHAT IS THE BUDDHA?	39
A MOTHER'S ADVICE	40
AṄGULIMĀLA AND THE DIFFICULT DELIVERY	41
A PILE OF DRY SHIT	43
THE MOST PROFOUND TEACHING	45
THE TRULY WISE OLD MONK	46
HOLY ANCESTORS	48
WHAT IS THE BUDDHA?	49
BUDDHA AND TAO	51
WHO IS THE BUDDHA?	52
WORDS	53

NAME OF AMIDA BUDDHA 55
WHAT DOES THE BUDDHA LOOK LIKE? 57
LU TSU FACES THE WALL 58
REJECTING YOUR FATHER 59
GO! 60
THE MEANING 61
FOUR GREAT VOWS 62
CH'IEN-YUAN'S PAPER SCREEN 63
HUI-CHUNG EXPELS HIS DISCIPLE 64
WHO IS HE? 65
YOU ARE SIDE-TRACKED 66
DEVIL TEACHINGS 67
TO STOP THE BABY CRYING 68
THE PLUM IS RIPE 69
THE PLACE 70
MYSTERY 71
THE BUDDHA-NATURE 72
HOW TO RUB MY EYES? 73
GO BACK 74
ANY FAULT? 75
BASO'S "THIS VERY MIND IS THE BUDDHA"
.... 76
KILL THE BUDDHA 77
THE CARDINAL PRINCIPLE 78

THE GREAT CROSSING	79
AN INSOLENT WAYFARER	80
THE MEANING	82
UNDERSTANDING THE DHARMA	83
THE GREAT MEANING	84
WHERE DID YOU COME FROM?	85
THE SUTRAS	86
WIFE AND CHILDREN	87
OPEN YOUR OWN TREASURE HOUSE	89
THE TRUE BODY	91
EXPOSED	92
THE WAY OF AWAKENING	93
THE OTHER BUDDHA	94
A ZEN DIALOGUE	96
WHO IS THE TEACHER OF ALL BUDDHAS?	97
BUDDHA IS AFFLICTION	98
THE GENUINE BUDDHA	99
WHEN?	100
THE TEACHING	101
THE GREAT MEANING	102
THERE IS NO BUDDHA	103
THE ESSENTIAL MEANING	104
DON'T STUDY THE WORDS OF BUDDHAS	105
SOUND OF BUDDHA	107

GET OUT!	108
HUANGBO BOWS TO A BUDDHA IMAGE	109
THE SECRET	110
THE DECEPTIVE BUDDHA	112
I ASK YOU	114
LIFE AND DEATH	115
WHO ARE BUDDHAS?	116
DO YOU UNDERSTAND?	117
THE ESSENTIAL MEANING	118
THE WHISK	119
SONG OF ENLIGHTENMENT	120
BUDDHA, A CLUMP OF DIRT	121
DONKEY	122
BLIND, DEAF AND MUTE	123
HEY YOU	124
CLARITY	125
THE ANCIENT BUDDHAS	126
UNDERSTANDING	127
THE LAST POEM	128
LOOK AND LISTEN	129
HELP!	130
REFLECTION	131
THE STRANGE LECTURE	132
THE ATTENDANT	134

THE SUPPORT	135
COMPLETE AWAKENING	136
THE BUDDHAS	137
THE ORDER	138
CRYING BABIES	139
AS THE BUDDHAS SAW	140
INSUFFICIENT	142
THE MEANING	143
ZEN	144
THE BUDDHA	145
ENLIGHTENMENT WITHIN DELUSION	146
KILL THE BUDDHA	147
DAYI'S "NO MIND"	148
ANGRY BUDDHA	149
YOU SPIT, I BOW	151
BUDDHAS DO NOT KNOW	152
THE BURNING HOUSE	153
UMMON'S STAFF	154
THE GREAT MEANING	155
LION CUB AND DONKEY	156
CAST OFF THE BUDDHA	157
THE PLACE	158
BEYOND BUDDHA	159
CALLING	160

DEAD FROGS 161
THE NIGHT INTERVIEW OF THE NUN
MYOTEI 162
WHAT IS NOT BUDDHA DHARMA? 165
YOU MONK TALKATIVE 166
THE BUDDHA 167
THE WORD: BUDDHA 169
DONGSHAN'S "GOING BEYOND BUDDHA"
.... 170
HESHAN BEATS THE DRUM 171
TOUZI ANSWERS "BUDDHA" 172
BUDDHA: THE EMPTINESS OF HEART 173
XUEFENG'S "TURNING THE DHARMA
WHEEL" 176
DAGUI'S "NO BUDDHA NATURE" 177
BUDDHA'S BEGGING BOWL 179
FAYAN'S "YOU ARE HUICHAO" 180
THE WORLD-HONORED ONE DID NOT
SPEAK A WORD 181
THE BUDDHAS 182
THE WOMAN AT THE INN 183
UNDERSTANDING 185
ESSENCE OF THE BUDDHA'S TEACHING .. 186
NO STUDY 187
THE WAY 188

DUMB 189
THE BUDDHA IN THE HOME 190
HARD 191
FORGETTING SLEEP AND FOOD 192
THE TATHĀGATA 193
NOTHING ATTAINED, NOTHING SPOKEN
.... 194
NOTHING SPOKEN 195
AND THE FLOWERS SHOWERED 196
VERBAL TEACHINGS 197
LOOKING FOR BUDDHAS 198
THE WAY OF BUDDHAS AND ZEN MASTERS
.... 199
NOT SEEKING 200
PITY 201
BUDDHA 202
THE PURE LIGHT 203
EVERYWHERE 204
SAME OR DIFFERENT? 205
SAME OR DIFFERENT? 206
THE SOURCE 207
BUDDHA 208
YUANWU'S "GATE OF MISFORTUNE" 209
SECRET 210

THE FUNDAMENTAL TEACHING 211
STRIKING THE BUDDHA 212
HEEDFULNESS 213
UNDERSTANDING OF BUDDHA...................214
THE ULTIMATE TEACHING 215
WHO IS THAT PERSON? 216
ZEN 217
WHAT IS BUDDHA? 218
THE BUDDHA-NATURE...................................219
TONGUE 220
THE BUDDHA 221
THE PRINCIPAL THRUST 222
THE BUDDHAS 223
THE BUDDHA-DHARMA.................................224
THE BUDDHA 225
THE MAIN PURPORT 226
THE MIND OF ANCIENT BUDDHAS 227
THE MAIN THRUST..228
THE MEANING 229
THE QUESTION 230
HOW MANY TIMES? 231
THE BUDDHA 232
THE POINTER...233
WHO TO ASK?...234

NOT KNOWN	235
CRAZY FELLOW	236
WHAT IS NOT?	237
THE MEANING	238
THE BUDDHA	239
EVADING	240
DEATH POEMS	241
THE STICK	243
KILL THE BUDDHA	244
THE BUDDHA	245
THE SOURCE	246
THE BUDDHA	247
OBSCURE AND DISTANT	248
PRACTICE	249
NOTHING ATTAINED	250
BIBLIOGRAPHY	251

THE TRUE HOMAGE

Zen Master Rinzai arrived at Bodhidharma's memorial tower. The master of the tower said to him, "Venerable sir, will you pay homage first to the Buddha or to Bodhidharma?"

"I don't pay homage to either the Buddha or to Bodhidharma," said Rinzai.

"Venerable sir, why are the Buddha and Bodhidharma your enemies?" asked the master of the tower.

Rinzai swung his sleeves and left.

~ The Record of Rinzai ~

SHAKYAMUNI WAS AN ORDINARY OLD FELLOW

Zen master Danxia Tianran entered the hall and addressed the monks, saying, "All of you here must take care of the temple and monastery. Things in this place were not made or named by you, and have they not been given as offerings? Formerly I studied with Shitou, and he taught me that I must personally protect these things. This is not to be discussed further.

"Each of you here has a place to put your cushion and sit. Why do you suspect you need something else? Is Zen something you can explain? Is a Buddha something you can become? I don't want to hear a single word about Buddhism.

"All of you look and see! Skilful means and expedience, the unlimited mind of benevolence, compassion, joy, and detachment-these things aren't received from someplace else. Not an inch of these things is evident. Skilful means is Manjushri Bodhisattva. Expedience is Samantabhadra Bodhisattva. Do you still want to go seeking after something? Don't go using the Buddhist scriptures to look for emptiness!

"These days Zen students are all in a tizzy, practicing Zen and asking about Tao. I don't have any Dharma for you to practice here! And there isn't any doctrine to be confirmed. Just eat and drink. Everyone can do that. Don't harbor doubt. It's the same everyplace!

"Just recognize that Shakyamuni was an ordinary old fellow. You must see for yourself. Don't spend your life trying to win some competitive trophy, blindly misleading other blind people, all of you marching right into hell, floundering in duality! I've nothing more to say. Take care!"

~ Zen's Chinese Heritage by Andy Ferguson ~

THE LIAR BUDDHA

If a Buddha would not speak, then people would have no hope of liberation; but if a Buddha speaks, then people pursue the words and create interpretations, so there would be little advantage and much disadvantage. That is why the Buddha said, "I would rather not explain the truth, but enter into extinction right away."
But then afterward he thought back on all the Buddhas of the past, who had all taught the doctrines of three vehicles. After that he made temporary use of verses to explain, and provisionally established names and terms. Originally it is not Buddha, but he told people, "This is Buddha." Originally it is not enlightenment, but he told people, "This is enlightenment, peace, liberation," and so on. He knew people couldn't bear a burden of ten thousand pounds, so for the time being he taught them the incomplete teaching. And he realized the spread of good ways, which was still better than evil ways.
But when the limits of good results are fulfilled, then bad consequences ensue. Once you have "Buddha," then there are sentient beings." Once you have "nirvana," then there is "birth and death." Once you have light, then there is darkness. As long as cause and effect with attachment continue to operate, there is nothing that does not have consequences.

~ Zen Master Baizhang Huaihai (720-814) ~
~ The Zen Reader, by Thomas Cleary ~

THE MISGUIDER BUDDHA

Shakyamuni,
That mischievous creature,
Having appeared in the world,
Misled, alas,
How many people!

Tell a lie,
And you fall into hell.
Then what will happen to Buddha
Who contrived things
That don't exist?

~ Zen Master Ikkyu ~
~ Take It Easy, Vol 1, by Osho ~

KILL THE BUDDHA

Chikamasa was a pupil of the well-known master Ikkyu Sojun (1394-1481). According to folklore, Chikamasa was greeted at the hour of his death by the three Buddhas of the past, the present, and the future, riding on purple clouds with twenty-five escorts. Chikamasa first ordered his son to bring him his weapons, then shot an arrow at the Buddha in the center. The warrior thus showed his contempt for the celestial retinue and his unconcern for the world to come. Before his death, Chikamasa said this poem:

Umarenuru
sono akatsuki ni
shininureba
kyō no yūbe wa
akikaze zo fuku

Meaning:

One day you are born
you die the next—
today,
at twilight,
autumn breezes blow.

~ Japanese Death Poems by Yoel Hoffmann ~

BUDDHA: THE DRIED PIECE OF EXCREMENT

Zen Master Deshan (Hsuan Chien, 782-865) entered the hall and addressed the monks, saying, "I see differently from our ancestors. Here there is neither Patriarch nor Buddha. Bodhidharma is an old stinking foreigner. Shakyamuni is a dried piece of excrement. Manjushri and Samantabhadra are dung-heap coolies. What is known as 'realizing the mystery' is nothing but breaking through to grab an ordinary person's life. Bodhi and Nirvana are nothing but dead stumps to tie the donkeys to. The twelve divisions of the scriptures are only registers of ghosts; just sheets of paper fit only for wiping the pus from your ulcers and tumours. All the 'four fruitions' and 'ten stages' are nothing but demons lingering in their decayed graves, who cannot even save themselves. They'll never save you."
"The wise seek not the Buddha. The Buddha is the great murderer who has seduced so many people into the pitfall of the prostituting Devil. "The old Barbarian rascal (the Buddha) claims that he had survived the destruction of three worlds. Where is he now? Did he not also die after 80 years of age? Was he in any way different from you? O ye wise men, disengage your body and your mind! Give up all and free yourself from all bondages."
"Here in my place, there is not a single truth for you to take home. I myself don't know what Zen is. I am no teacher, knowing nothing at all. I am only an old beggar who begs his food and clothing and

daily moves his bowels. What else have I to do? But allow me to tell you: Have nothing to do: go and take an early rest!"

~ Zen's Chinese Heritage by Andy Ferguson ~

TALK WITHIN A DREAM

Zen master Panshan entered the hall and addressed the monks, saying, "Zen worthies! ...Transcendent wisdom is not clear. True emptiness leaves no trace. 'True thusness,' 'mundane,' and 'sacred,' are all just talk within a dream. 'Buddha' and 'nirvana' are just extra words.
Zen worthies! Directly observe for yourself! No one can do it for you!"

~ Zen's Chinese Heritage by Andy Ferguson ~

BLACK-NOSED BUDDHA

A nun who was searching for enlightenment made a statue of Buddha and covered it with gold leaf. Wherever she went she carried this golden Buddha with her.

Years passed and, still carrying her Buddha, the nun came to live in a small temple in a country where there were many Buddhas, each one with its own particular shrine.

The nun wished to burn incense before her golden Buddha. Not liking the idea of the perfume straying to others, she devised a funnel through which the smoke would ascend only to her statue. This blackened the nose of the golden Buddha, making it especially ugly.

~ Zen Flesh, Zen Bones by Nyogen Senzaki and Paul Reps~

THE TEACHING OF THE WHOLE LIFETIME

A monk asked Zen Master Unmon, "What is the teaching of the whole lifetime of Shakyamuni?"

Unmon said, "Preaching one thing."

~ Case 14 of Hekiganroku ~

THE LAST WILL AND TESTAMENT

Ikkyu, a famous Zen teacher of the Ashikaga era, was the son of the emperor. When he was very young, his mother left the palace and went to study Zen in a temple. In this way Prince Ikkyu also became a student. When this mother passed on, she left him a letter. It read:

To Ikkyu:

I have finished my work in this life and am now returning into Eternity. I wish you to become a good student and to realize your Buddha-nature. You will know if I am in hell and whether I am always with you or not.

If you become a man who realizes that the Buddha and his follower Bodhidharma are your own servants, you may leave off studying and work for humanity. The Buddha preached for forty-nine years and in all that time found it not necessary to speak one word. You ought to know why. But if you don't and yet wish to, avoid thinking fruitlessly.

Your Mother,

Not born, not dead.

September first.

P.S. *The teaching of Buddha was mainly for the purpose of enlightening others. If you are dependent on any of its methods, you are naught but an ignorant insect. There are 80,000 books on Buddhism and if you should read all of them and still not see your own nature, you will not understand even this letter. This is my will and testament.*

~ Zen Flesh, Zen Bones by Nyogen Senzaki and Paul Reps~

THE MOST IMPORTANT TEACHING

A renowned Zen master said that his greatest teaching was this: Buddha is your own mind. So impressed by how profound this idea was, one monk decided to leave the monastery and retreat to the wilderness to meditate on this insight. There he spent 20 years as a hermit probing the great teaching.

One day he met another monk who was traveling through the forest. Quickly the hermit monk learned that the traveller also had studied under the same Zen master. "Please, tell me what you know of the master's greatest teaching." The traveller's eyes lit up, "Ah, the master has been very clear about this. He says that his greatest teaching is this: Buddha is NOT your own mind."

~ Zen Flesh, Zen Bones by Nyogen Senzaki and Paul Reps~

ZEN TEACHINGS OF BODHIDHARMA

- Trying to find a Buddha or enlightenment is like trying to grab space.

- Buddhas of the past and future only talk about this mind. The mind is the Buddha, and the Buddha is the mind. Beyond the mind there's no Buddha and beyond the Buddha there's no mind. If you think there is a Buddha beyond the mind', where is he? There's no Buddha beyond the mind, so why envision one? You can't know your real mind as long as you deceive yourself. As long as you're enthralled by a lifeless form, you're not free. If you don't believe me, deceiving yourself won't help. It's not the Buddha's fault. People, though, are deluded. They're unaware that their own mind is the Buddha. Otherwise they wouldn't look for a Buddha outside the mind.

- If you use your mind to look for a Buddha, you won't see the Buddha. As long as you look for a Buddha somewhere else, you'll never see that your own mind is the Buddha. Don't use a Buddha to worship a Buddha. And don't use the mind to invoke a Buddha." Buddhas don't recite sutras." Buddhas don't keep precepts." And

Buddhas don't break precepts. Buddhas don't keep or break anything. Buddhas don't do good or evil.

- To find a Buddha, you have to see your nature. Whoever sees his nature is a Buddha. If you don't see your nature, invoking Buddhas, reciting sutras, making offerings, and keeping precepts are all useless.

- To find a Buddha all you have to do is see your nature. Your nature is the Buddha. And the Buddha is the person who's free: free of plans, free of cares. If you don't see your nature and run around all day looking somewhere else, you'll never find a buddha. The truth is there's nothing to find. But to reach such an understanding you need a teacher and you need to struggle to make yourself understand.

- Unless they see their nature, how can people call themselves Buddhas they're liars who deceive others into entering the realm of devils. Unless they see their nature, their preaching of the Twelvefold Canon is nothing but the preaching of devils. Their allegiance is to Mara, not to the Buddha. Unable to distinguish white from black, how can they escape birth and death?

- Whoever sees his nature is a buddha; whoever doesn't is a mortal. But if you can find your buddha-nature apart from your mortal nature, where is it? Our mortal nature is our buddha nature. Beyond this nature there's no Buddha. The Buddha is our nature. There's no buddha besides this nature. And there's no nature besides the Buddha.

- To say he attains anything at all is to slander a Buddha. What could he possibly attain?

- A Buddha doesn't observe precepts. A Buddha doesn't do good or evil. A Buddha isn't energetic or lazy. A Buddha is someone who does nothing, someone who can't even focus his mind on a Buddha. A Buddha isn't a Buddha. Don't think about Buddhas. If you don't see what I'm talking about, you'll ever know your own mind.

- If you envision a Buddha, a Dharma, or a bodhisattva" and conceive respect for them, you relegate yourself to the realm of mortals. If you seek direct understanding, don't hold on to any appearance whatsoever, and you'll succeed. I have no other advice. The sutras say, "All appearances are illusions." They have no fixed existence, o constant form. They're impermanent. Don't cling to appearances and you'll be of one mind with the Buddha. The sutras say, "'That which is free of all form is the Buddha."

~ The Zen Teaching of Bodhidharma, Translated by Red Pine ~

NOTHING EXISTS

Yamaoka Tesshu, as a young student of Zen, visited one master after another. He called upon Dokuon of Shokoku.

Desiring to show his attainment, he said: "The mind, Buddha, and sentient beings, after all, do not exist. The true nature of phenomena is emptiness. There is no realization, no delusion, no sage, no mediocrity. There is no giving and nothing to be received."

Dokuon, who was smoking quietly, said nothing. Suddenly he whacked Yamaoka with his bamboo pipe. This made the youth quite angry.

"If nothing exists," inquired Dokuon, "where did this anger come from?"

~ Zen Flesh, Zen Bones by Nyogen Senzaki and Paul Reps~

A PHILOSOPHER ASKS BUDDHA

A philosopher asked Buddha: `Without words, without the wordless, will you tell me truth?'
The Buddha kept silence.
The philosopher bowed and thanked the Buddha, saying: `With your loving kindness I have cleared away my delusions and entered the true path.'
After the philosopher had gone, Ananda asked the Buddha what he had attained.
The Buddha replied, `A good horse runs even at the shadow of the whip.'

~ Mumonkan, The Gateless Gate, by Ekai, called Mu-mon, tr. Nyogen Senzaki and Paul Reps ~

BUDDHA TWIRLS A FLOWER

Buddha was to give a special talk one day on the Vulture Peak (Grdhrakuta Mountain), and thousands of followers had come from miles around. When Buddha appeared, he was holding a flower. Time passed, but Buddha said nothing. He just looked at the flower. The crowd grew restless, but Mahākāśyapa, who could restrain himself no longer, laughed. Buddha beckoned him over, handed him the flower, and said to the crowd, "I have the eye of the true teaching. All that can be given with words I have given to you; but with this flower, I give to Mahākāśyapa the key to this teaching."

~A Bird on the Wing by Osho. This is also Case 6 of Mumonkan and Case 135 of Entangling Vines ~

THE MEANING

Zen Master Baeg-un (1299-1375) instructed the assembly, saying, "At the assembly on Mt. Grdhrakūta, the World Honored picked up a flower, and the great assembly of billions of humans and gods were all totally at a loss, and only Mahākāśyapa personally perceived (the Buddha's intent) and so broke into a smile. Now say, what matter did Kāśyapa personally perceive? You should not say, 'The Tathāgata spoke by not speaking, Kāśyapa perceived by not perceiving,' or something like, 'The Tathāgata had a secret language and Kāśyapa did not hide it.' The World Honored also said, 'I have a storehouse of the eye of the Correct Dharma that I confer on Mahākāśyapa.' What is this? Even though it is so, I say, 'At Mt. Grdhrakūta (the Buddha) spoke of the moon; at Cao Creek (Hui-Neng) pointed at the moon.'"

~ (Collected Works of Korean Buddhism, Volume 8) Seon Dialogues, Edited and Translated by John Jorgensen ~

NO TRANSMISSION

Zen master Baiyun Shouduan entered the hall and addressed the monks, saying, "In former times there was an assembly at Vulture Peak where the World-Honored One held up a flower, and Mahākāśyapa smiled. The World-Honored One said, 'I have The Treasury of the True Dharma Eye. I pass it to Mahākāśyapa.' This was then passed on in succession down to the present day.
I say to this assembly that if it was really the true Dharma eye, then old Shakyamuni didn't have it, and so how could he have passed it on? How could it have been transmitted? How can such a thing be said?"

~ Zen's Chinese Heritage by Andy Ferguson ~

DESHAN'S "ASSEMBLY ON VULTURE PEAK"

Deshan Dehai was once asked by a monastic, "Who was able to hear Shakyamuni Buddha at the assembly on Vulture Peak?"

Deshan said, "The venerable heard it."

The monastic said, "I wonder what was spoken at the assembly on Vulture Peak?"

Deshan said, "The venerable understands it."

[NOTE: The question is: Who is this venerable?]

~ Dogen's 300 Koans ~

THE WORLD-HONORED ONE ASCENDS THE TEACHING SEAT

One day the World-Honored One ascended the teaching seat and the assembly came together.

Mahākāśyapa struck the mallet and announced: "The World-Honored One has just expounded the dharma."

The World-Honored One descended from the teaching seat.

~ Dogen's 300 Koans~

A BUDDHA BEFORE HISTORY

A monk asked Seijo: `I understand that a Buddha who lived before recorded history sat in meditation for ten cycles of existence and could not realize the highest truth, and so could not become fully emancipated. Why was this so?'
Seijo replied: `Your question is self-explanatory.'
The monk asked: `Since the Buddha was meditating, why could he not fulfill Buddhahood?'
Seijo said: `He was not a Buddha.'

~ Mumonkan, The Gateless Gate, by Ekai, called Mu-mon, tr. Nyogen Senzaki and Paul Reps ~

TOZAN'S THREE POUNDS

A monk asked Tozan when he was weighing some flax: `What is Buddha?'
Tozan said: `These flax weighs three pounds.'

~ Mumonkan, The Gateless Gate, by Ekai, called Mu-mon, tr. Nyogen Senzaki and Paul Reps; also, Case 12 of Hekiganroku (The Blue Cliff Record) ~

DRIED DUNG

A monk asked Ummon: "What is Buddha?"
Ummon answered him: "Dried dung."

~ Mumonkan, The Gateless Gate, by Ekai, called Mu-mon, tr. Nyogen Senzaki and Paul Reps ~

NOT MIND, NOT BUDDHA, NOT THINGS

A monk asked Nansen: 'Is there a teaching no master ever preached before?'
Nansen said: 'Yes, there is.'
'What is it?' asked the monk.
Nansen replied: 'It is not mind, it is not Buddha, it is not things.'

~ Mumonkan, The Gateless Gate, by Ekai, called Mu-mon, tr. Nyogen Senzaki and Paul Reps ~

MAZU'S "MIND IS BUDDHA"

Damei Fachang asked Mazu, "What is Buddha?"

Mazu said, "Mind is Buddha."

~ Dogen's 300 Koans ~

YOU ARE ALREADY A BUDDHA

An old Zen story tells of a pilgrim who mounted his horse and crossed formidable mountains and swift rivers seeking a famous wise man in order to ask him how to find true enlightenment. After months of searching, the pilgrim located the teacher in a cave.

The Master listened to the question and said nothing. The seeker waited. Finally, after hours of silence, the Master looked at the steed on which the pilgrim had arrived, and asked the pilgrim why he was not looking for a horse instead of enlightenment.

The pilgrim responded that obviously he already had a horse. The Master smiled, and retreated into his cave. Very indicative! The Master said," Why don't you search for a horse? Why do you bother about Buddhahood?"

And the man said," What nonsense are you talking about? The horse is already with me. I have got the horse! Why should I seek it?"

And the Master didn't say anything – he simply smiled and retreated into his cave. Finished! He had given the answer.

You are a Buddha. You cannot search for it. That is the great declaration of all the great religions – that you are gods and goddesses in disguise, incognito.

You have forgotten your own identity; you don't know who you are. Hence all seeking. And sometimes you start seeking that which you are already. Then it is impossible to find... then frustration.

Don't start seeking, just start looking at what is the case. Looking into the reality as it is, is enough. That is the meaning of Zen people when they say" Be here now" – look into reality.

Nothing is missing, all is already here. Listening to it, please avoid creating an ideal; otherwise your ideal will mislead you.

~ Zen: The Path of Paradox, Vol 3 by Osho ~

MANJUSRI ENTERS THE GATE

One day as Manjusri stood outside the gate, the Buddha called to him, "Manjusri, Manjusri, why do you not enter?"

Manjusri replied, "I do not see myself as outside. Why enter?"

~ The Iron Flute: 100 Zen Koans by Nyogen Senzaki, Ruth Strout-McCandless ~

BAOFU'S BLOCKING OF THE EYES, EARS, AND MIND

Dizang asked a monastic from Baofu Monastery, "How does your master teach the Buddhadharma?"

The monastic said, "Once Master Baofu Congzhan told the assembly, 'I cover your eyes to let you see what is not seen. 2I cover your ears to let you hear what is not heard. I restrain your mind to let you give up thinking.'"

Dizang said to the monastic, "Let me ask you, when I don't cover your eyes, what do you see? When I don't cover your ears, what do you hear? When I don't restrain your mind, what do you discern?"

Upon hearing these words, the monastic had realization.

~ Dogen's 300 Koans ~

JOSHU AND THE GREAT BUDDHA

When he was a teenager, Joshu studied under Nansen. Nansen asked him: "Where did you come from?"

"I am from Zuizo," he said.

"Did you pray to the Great Buddha in Zuizo?" asked Nansen.

"No sir, the Great Buddha is in front of me, lying down on the floor."

"What are you talking about?" asked Nansen.

"My great teacher," Joshu said, "I am so pleased to see that you are in good spirits and good health."

~ Adapted from Treasury of the Forest of Ancestors by Satyavayu and The Original Teachings of Ch'an Buddhism by Chang Ching Yuan ~

WHO'S THE BUDDHA?

Yu-ti asked Tao-t'ing: "Who is the Buddha?"

Tao-t'ing called out: "Oh, Yu-ti!"

"Yes, master?" Yu-ti responded.

Whereupon the Master said: "Don't seek him elsewhere."

~ The Zen Doctrine of No-Mind by D. T. Suzuki~

THE AIM

A long time ago, Baso of Kiangsi Province was training under Zen Master Nangaku. While staying in Chuan-fa Temple, Baso had been doing seated meditation day in and day out for some ten years or more.

One day when Nangaku came to Baso's hut, Baso stood up to receive him. Nangaku asked him, "What have you been doing recently?"

Baso replied, "Recently I have been doing the practice of seated meditation exclusively."

Nangaku asked, "And what is the aim of your meditation?"

Baso replied, "The aim of my seated meditation is to achieve Buddhahood."

Thereupon, Nangaku took a roof tile and began rubbing it on a rock near Baso's hut.

Baso, upon seeing this, asked him, "Reverend Monk, what are you doing?"

Nangaku replied, "I am polishing a roof tile."

Baso then asked, "What are you going to make by polishing a roof tile?"

Nangaku replied, "I am polishing it to make a mirror."

Baso said, "How can you possibly make a mirror by rubbing a tile?"

Nangaku replied, "How can you possibly make yourself into a Buddha by doing meditation?"

[NOTE: This story is taken from the book **Shobogenzo**, written by the great Zen Master Dogen! The translator says:

The translation may not clearly convey the contradiction in Baso's statement. The particular practice of seated meditation he specifically mentions is 'chih-kuan ta-tsuo', a Chinese colloquial phrase that implies sitting in meditation without deliberately thinking of anything, or holding on to anything that naturally arises, or pushing away anything that naturally arises, and without trying to suppress any thoughts from arising. However, in reply to Nangaku's question, Baso indicates that, in fact, he has something he is deliberately holding in his mind, namely, the goal of realizing Buddhahood, literally 'making himself into a Buddha'!]

Dogen said:
Polishing a tile to make a mirror is diligent effort.
and
Polishing a tile to make a mirror is our reward for accumulating merit and virtue.
He also said:
Instead of hitting the ox, you should hit the cart.
and When one cart is hit, many carts go quickly.

WHAT IS THE BUDDHA?

A monk asked Joshu: "What is the Buddha?"

"The one in the hall."

The monk said, "The one in the hall is a statue, a lump of mud."

Joshu said, "That's so."

"What is the Buddha, then?" asked the monk again.

"The one in the hall," said Joshu.

~ A Sudden Clash of Thunder by Osho ~

A MOTHER'S ADVICE

Jiun, a Shogun master, was a well-known Sanskrit scholar of the Tokugawa era. When he was young, he used to deliver lectures to his brother students.

His mother heard about this and wrote him a letter:

"Son, I do not think you became a devotee of the Buddha because you desired to turn into a walking dictionary for others. There is no end to information and commentation, glory and honor. I wish you would stop this lecture business. Shut yourself up in a little temple in a remote part of the mountain. Devote your time to meditation and in this way attain true realization."

~ Zen Flesh, Zen Bones by Nyogen Senzaki and Paul Reps~

AṄGULIMĀLA AND THE DIFFICULT DELIVERY

Once Aṅgulimāla went into a city with his begging bowl and came to the home of a rich man. At the time the wealthy man's wife was going through a difficult delivery. The wealthy man asked Aṅgulimāla, "Śramaṇa, you are a disciple of the Buddha. Is there some way in which to spare my wife this difficult delivery?"

Aṅgulimāla replied, "I have only recently entered the Way and don't yet know such a method. I will immediately return to the Buddha, ask him, then come and tell you." He hurried back and related the above matter to the Buddha.

The Buddha told him, "Go quickly and tell him, 'Since coming to know the wise and holy Dharma, never once have I taken life.'"[1]

Following the Buddha's advice, Aṅgulimāla went back to the rich man and told him this. The moment the man's wife heard this; she gave birth to her child. The mother and child were safe.

NOTE

1. Prior to joining the sangha and becoming a monk, Aṅgulimāla had been a notorious mass murderer.

~ Entangling Vines: A Classic Collection of Zen Koans by Thomas Yuho Kirchner~

A PILE OF DRY SHIT

One day a famous government officer met a highly respected elderly master. Being conceited, he wanted to prove that he was the superior person.

As their conversation drew on, he asked the master, "Old monk, do you know what I think of you and the things you said?"

The master replied, "I don't care what you think of me. You are entitled to have your own opinion."

The officer snorted, "Well, I will tell you what I think anyway. In my eyes, you are just like a pile of dry shit!"

The master simply smiled and stayed quiet.

Seeing that his insult had fallen into deaf ears, he asked curiously, "And what do you think of me?"

The master said, "In my eyes, you are just like the Buddha."

Hearing this remark, the officer left happily and bragged to his wife about the incident.

His wife said to him, "You conceited fool! When a person has a heart like a pile of dry shit, he sees everyone in that light. The elderly master has a heart like that of the Buddha, and that is why in his eyes, everyone, including you, is like the Buddha!"

~ Once Upon a Time: A Collection of Buddhist Stories

(http://www.sinc.sunysb.edu/Clubs/buddhism/story/dryshit.html)~

THE MOST PROFOUND TEACHING

Bai Juyi (772-846 CE) was an important poet and government officer during the Tang Dynasty in China. He once asked a Buddhist monk for the most essential Dharma instruction, and the monk replied by quoting the Buddha's summary teaching, "Avoid harm. Do good. Purify the mind by meditation."

Bai Juyi was not impressed, "Every child of three years knows these words. What I want to know is the most profound and fundamental teaching of the Buddha."

The monk replied, "Every child of three years knows these words, but white-haired men of eighty still fail to put them into practice."

~ Source: Unknown ~

THE TRULY WISE OLD MONK

A young Zen monk was recognized by his teacher as having experienced an initial breakthrough enlightenment (Japanese: satori, kensho). His teacher then told the young man that, for realizing complete, irreversible enlightenment (Sanskrit: anuttara-samyakasambodhi), he would need to study under a certain wise old master whose small temple was situated in another part of the country. And so, the young man set off to meet the old master. After several weeks of travel, he finally arrived at the remote temple. The sentry told him that all the other monks were working at their daily chores, and sent the young man straightaway to the meditation hall to meet the venerable master.

Entering the meditation hall, the young monk espied an old man doing repeated prostrations to a simple statue of the Buddha, softly chanting the name of Buddha Amida (who saves all sentient beings from suffering). The young man was shocked. Having realized from his teacher the basic truth that the Self or Buddha-nature is formless openness-emptiness, utterly transcendent and all-pervasive, he was a bit disturbed to see the old man apparently still caught up in such "dualistic" practices—ritually bowing to an idol and chanting with devotion to a mythical Buddha.

And so, he came up to the aged monk, introduced himself, and, from his "truly enlightened" perspective, proceeded to lecture the old man on the futility and stupidity of worshipping mere forms. Finally, his brief rant over, he realized that, having travelled such a long way to meet the "master," he should probably ask the old monk for whatever wisdom he had to share. "So, old man, what can you tell me about full enlightenment?"

In response, the master smiled, said nothing, and resumed sincerely bowing in gratitude before the statue of the Buddha, gently invoking the Name of Amida on behalf of all beings....

And, in a flash, the young man fully understood the way of true spirituality, and he, too, began spontaneously to bow alongside the old master.

~ Zen Humor: Classic Humor from the Zen - Chan - Son Buddhist Tradition by Timothy Conway ~

HOLY ANCESTORS

A monk asked Zen Master Feng of Guoqing monastery in Longzhou (Shanxi, Long xian), "What is the basic meaning of the Buddha-dharma?"

"Shakyamuni is the prison guard with the bull's head, the masters and patriarchs are the horse-faced," replied the master.

[Note: The Lord of Avici Hell has two prison guards - one with a bull's head and a man's body, his two legs like a bull's hind legs, the arms with iron claws; the other had a horse's head and a man's body and is called 'horse head'. (Mentioned in the Lankavatara Sutra)]

~ Records of the Transmission of the Lamp (Jingde Chuandeng Lu) by Daoyuan, Vol. 3, Translated by Randolph S Whitfield ~

WHAT IS THE BUDDHA?

Different Zen Masters have answered this question in different way:

Zen Master Baiyun: "A hot soup pot has no cool spot."

Zen Master Shouchu: "The crystal-clear truth."

Zen Master Zhimen: "When the straw sandals are worn out, continue barefoot."

Zen Master Dong-Sahn: "Three pounds of cloth."

Zen Master Un-Mon: "Dry shit on a stick."

Zen Master Duck-Sahn: Hit.

Zen Master Im-Je: "KATZ!"

Zen Master Ku-Ji: One finger.

Zen Master Man Gong: A circle made with the fingers.

Zen Master JoJu: "Go drink tea."

Zen Master Keang-Ho: "Did you wash your bowl?"

Zen Master Ma Jo:

1. "Mind is Buddha."

2. "No mind is no Buddha."

Zen Master Hea Jo: "Did you eat before you came here?"

Guizong said: "When I tell you it becomes something else."

Zen master Yanzhao of Fengxue: "At the foot of the bamboo forested mountain the stems grow like whips."

Touzi Daitong (T'ou-tzu Tai-t'ung, d.914), a mentor to famous Chan master Zhaozhou (Chao-chou), was once asked, "What is the Buddha?" His considered response: "The Buddha!"

When Nanyuan Huiyong (860-930) was likewise asked (it's a very popular question in Chan tradition!), "What is the Buddha?" He replied, "What is not the Buddha?" Another time his answer was, "I never knew him." On a third occasion, when asked "What is the Buddha?" — Nanyuan replied, "Wait until there is one — then I'll tell you."

SOURCES:
1. Records of the Transmission of The Lamp
2. Teaching Letters of Zen Master Seung Sahn
3. Zen Humor: Classic Humor from the Zen - Chan - Son Buddhist Tradition by Timothy Conway

BUDDHA AND TAO

In a Ming-time text, An Addition to the Record of the Transmission of the Lamp (Xu chuan deng lu) the idiom occurs as describing Ordinary Way. The ordinariness of the Way of Chan is often emphasized in the classical dialogues between a master and a student: the student asks a teacher about matters concerning Buddhist philosophy, and the master replies using extremely down-to earth sentences, such as "eat the food, wear the clothes".

Question: "What is Buddha?"

The master answers: "Wearing clothes, eating food.

A commoner asks: "What is Buddha?"

The master answers: "The way to homely wear one's clothes and eat one's food."

~ Talking about Food Doesn't Appease Hunger: Phrases on hunger in Chan (Zen) Buddhist texts by Anu Niemi ~

WHO IS THE BUDDHA?

A monk asked Chan master Baizhang (Pai-chang, 749-814), "Who is the Buddha?" Baizhang answered: "Who are you?"

~ Zen Humor: Classic Humor from the Zen - Chan - Son Buddhist Tradition by Timothy Conway~

WORDS

Some officials came to see the Chinese emigre Chan/Zen master Lanqi Daolong (J: Daikaku Zenji; 1213-78) of Kamakura, Japan, and complained that the one-page Hridaya Sutra ("Heart Scripture"), chanted daily in Zen monasteries, is too long and difficult to read. They preferred the 7-syllable mantra given by Nichiren of the New Lotus school (Namu Myoho Renge Kyo) or even the 6-syllable Nembutsu (Namu Amida Butsu) of the Pure Land Buddhist school. Daikaku listened to them and said, "If you want to recite the Zen scripture, do it with just one word. It is the six- and seven-syllable phrases which are far too long!"

Master Setsuo would present this story of Daikaku to his own pupils: "The Zen school says that the Buddha in all his 49 years of preaching never uttered a single word. But our Old Buddha (Daikaku) declares one word to lead the people to salvation. What is that word? What is that one great word?! If you cannot find it your whole life will be spent entangled in creepers in a dark cave. If you can say it, with that leap of realization you will pervade heaven and earth." Those to whom Setsuo gave this riddle over the years tried the word "Heart" and the word "Buddha," also the words "God," "Truth," "mantra," etc., but none of them hit it.

So, what is that one word?

~ Zen Humor: Classic Humor from the Zen - Chan - Son Buddhist Tradition by Timothy Conway~

NAME OF AMIDA BUDDHA

When, earlier in his ministry as a famous Zen Roshi, Takuan was asked by a monk whether he ever performed the sacred Nembutsu recitation of the holy Name of Amida Buddha, he replied, "No, never." "Why not?" "Because I don't want my mouth polluted!" Yet it's funny: Takuan had spent years in his youth involved in chanting Amida's name as a member of the Pure Land devotional Buddhist sect!

Later, in his little text Reiroshu, Takuan told the following story:

When Ippen Shonin (13th cent.; later a father of Pure Land Buddhism) met Zen master Hotto Kokushi, the founder of the Kokokuji Temple in Yura village, he said, "I have composed a poem." Master Kokushi said, "Let's hear it." Ippen recited:

When I chant,

Both Buddha and self

Cease to exist,

There is only the voice that says,

Namu Amida Butsu.

Kokushi said, "Something's wrong with the last couple of lines, don't you think?" Ippen then confined himself in Kumano and meditated for twenty-one days. When he passed by Yura again, he said to the Master, "This is how I've written it":

When I chant,

Both Buddha and self

Cease to exist.

Namu Amida Butsu,

Namu Amida Butsu.

Kokushi nodded his enthusiastic approval, "That's it!"

~ Zen Humor: Classic Humor from the Zen - Chan - Son Buddhist Tradition by Timothy Conway~

WHAT DOES THE BUDDHA LOOK LIKE?

Daoquan (Tao-ch'uan), a 12th century Chan master, wrote a verse:

Make it out of clay or wood or silk

paint it blue or green and gild it with gold

but if you think a buddha looks like this

the Goddess of Mercy (Guanyin) will die from laughter.

~ Zen Humor: Classic Humor from the Zen - Chan - Son Buddhist Tradition by Timothy Conway~

LU TSU FACES THE WALL

Whenever Lu Tsu saw a monk coming, he immediately sat facing the wall.

Hearing of this, his brother monk Nansen said, "I tell my monks to put themselves into the time before Buddhas appeared in the world, but few of them truly realize my Zen. Merely sitting against the wall like Brother Lu-tsu would never do the monks any good."

~Shoyoroku~

REJECTING YOUR FATHER

Zen master Shenxiu (606-706) had a verse that he recited to instruct the congregation:

All Buddha dharmas come forth fundamentally from mind.

If you waste effort seeking it outside,

It's like rejecting your father and running away from home.

~ Zen's Chinese Heritage by Andy Ferguson ~

GO!

A monk asked, "How does one speak of the great mystery?"

Daowu said, "Don't say 'I have realized the Buddhadharma!'"

The monk asked, "How do you deal with students who are stuck?"

Daowu said, "Why don't you ask me?"

The monk said, "I just asked you."

Daowu said, "Go! This isn't the place where you'll find relief."

~ Zen's Chinese Heritage by Andy Ferguson ~

THE MEANING

A monk asked, "What's the essential meaning of Zen?"
Zen Master Xita replied, "You don't have buddha nature."
The monk said, "What is sudden enlightenment?"
Xita drew a circle on the ground for the monk to see.
The monk asked, "What is gradual enlightenment?"
Xita poked the middle of the empty space three times with his hand.

~ Zen's Chinese Heritage by Andy Ferguson ~

FOUR GREAT VOWS

Zen Master Baiyun once said, "Old Shakyamuni recited four great vows, which were:

Though the myriad beings are numberless, I vow to save them;

Though defilements rise endlessly, I vow to end them;

Though Dharma gates are innumerable, I vow to study them;

Though Buddha's way is unsurpassed, I vow to embody it.

"I also have four great vows. They are:

When I'm hungry, I eat;

When it's cold, I put on more clothes;

When I'm tired, I stretch out and sleep;

When it gets warm, I like to find a cool breeze."

~ Zen's Chinese Heritage by Andy Ferguson ~

CH'IEN-YUAN'S PAPER SCREEN

Ch'ien-yuan, a master, sat behind a paper screen. A monk came for sanzen, lifted the screen, and greeted the teacher, "It is strange." The teacher gazed at the monk then said, "Do you understand?"

"No, I do not understand," the monk replied.

"Before the seven Buddhas appeared in the world," said the teacher, "it was the same as the present moment. Why do you not understand?"

Later the monk mentioned the incident to Shih-Shuang, a Zen teacher of the Dharma family, who praised Ch'ien-yuan, saying, "Brother Ch'ien-yuan is like a master archer. He never shot an arrow without hitting the mark."

~The Iron Flute: 100 Zen Koans by Nyogen Senzaki, Ruth Strout-McCandless~

HUI-CHUNG EXPELS HIS DISCIPLE

Tan-hsia paid a visit to Hui-chung, who was taking a nap at the time. "Is your teacher in?" asked Tan-hsia of an attending disciple. "Yes, he is, but he does not want to see anyone," said the monk. "You are expressing the situation profoundly," Tan-hsia said. "Don't mention it. Even if Buddha comes, my teacher does not want to see him." "You are certainly a good disciple. Your teacher ought to be proud of you," and with these words of praise, Tan-hsia left the temple. When Hui-chung awoke, Tan-yüan, the attending monk, repeated the dialogue. The teacher beat the monk with a stick and drove him from the temple.

~The Iron Flute: 100 Zen Koans by Nyogen Senzaki, Ruth Strout-McCandless~

WHO IS HE?

Zen Master Hoen said, "The past and future Buddhas, both are his servants. Who is he?"

~ Mumonkan, The Gateless Gate, by Ekai, called Mu-mon ~

YOU ARE SIDE-TRACKED

A Zen student told Unmon, "Brilliancy of Buddha illuminates the whole universe." Before he finished the phrase, Unmon asked,

"You are reciting another's poem, are you not?" "Yes," answered the student. "You are side-tracked," said Unmon. Afterward, another teacher, Shishin, asked his pupils, "At what point did that student go off the track?"

[Note by Venerable Gyomay M. Kubose: When one speaks honestly and sincerely, one should take the responsibility for one's words. Many people say "they say" or "men are" or "people talk" Instead, why doesn't one say "I am" or "I say"?]

~ Mumonkan, The Gateless Gate, by Ekai, called Mu-mon and Zen Koans by Venerable Gyomay M Kubose ~

DEVIL TEACHINGS

Zen Master Isan said to Kyozan, "The Nirvana Sutra has about forty chapters of the Buddha's teaching; how many of these are devil teachings?"

Kyozan said, "All of them."

Isan said, "From now on nobody will be able to do what he likes with you."

Kyozan said, "From now on what should be my mode of life?"

Isan said, "I admire your just eye [Dharma Eye?]; I am not concerned about the practical side of the matter."

~ Kyozan, A True Man of Zen by Osho ~

TO STOP THE BABY CRYING

A monk asked Baso, "Why do you teach this "The mind is the Buddha?"

Baso said, "To stop the baby crying."

The monk asked, "And when the baby stops crying?"

Baso said, "Mind is not the Buddha."

The monk asked, "Besides this, is there something more?"

Baso replied, "I will tell you; it is not something."

~ Zen and Zen Classics, Vol 3, by R.H. Blyth ~

THE PLUM IS RIPE

When Fa-chang (752-839 CE) of Mt. Ta-mei ("Great Plum") first visited the master, he inquired about the meaning of the word "Buddha."

"The Mind is Buddha," said Ma-tsu. Upon that Fa-chang was enlightened. Later Fa-chang retired once more to Ta-mei and taught others there. When the master heard of this, he dispatched a monk to inquire what it was that Fa-chang had so learned that allowed him to presume to head a mountain lineage. Fa-chang told the monk that it was the dictum, "The Mind is Buddha." The monk noted, "Recently the master sings a different tune. Now it is 'Neither Mind nor Buddha'."

Fa-chang reacted, "That rascal deludes people to no end! Let him teach you how there is neither mind nor Buddha. For my part, I will stick to 'The Mind is Buddha.'"

When the monk reported this to the master, Ma-tsu remarked, "Indeed, the plum is ripe."

~ Source: Unknown ~

THE PLACE

Once Chokoman was asked, "What is the place of religious exercises of the ancient Buddhas?"
Chokoman said, "Just by walking, they trod on it."
The monk went on, "And after they had trod on it?"
Chokoman replied, "Ice melting, tiles breaking up."
The monk then asked, "How does that happen?"
Chokoman responded by saying, "The gentlemen in the city, the little children outside the walls."

~ Zen: The Mystery and The Poetry of The Beyond by Osho ~

MYSTERY

A monk asked Ikan, a student of Baso, "Has the dog Buddha-nature or not?"
Ikan said, "Yes."
The monk asked, "Have you it or not?"
Ikan said, "I have not."
Monk: "All existent creatures have the Buddha-Natures; how is it that you have not?"
Ikan: "I don't belong to all existent creatures."
Monk: "You say you don't belong to all existent creatures. This 'You', is it a Buddha or not? "
Ikan: "It is not a Buddha."
Monk: "What sort of thing, in the last resort, is this 'You'?"
Ikan: "It is not a thing."
Monk: "Can it be perceived or thought of?"
Ikan: "Thought cannot attain to it; it cannot be fathomed. For this reason, it is said to be a mystery."

~ Mumonkan (Originally titled 'Zen and Zen Classics, Vol. 4'), Translated by R.H. Blyth [Commentary on Case 1] ~

THE BUDDHA-NATURE

There is an interesting story concerning Nyoe, 744-823, also a pupil of Baso.

As Saigun entered the temple, he noticed a sparrow making droppings on the head of an image of Buddha, and said to Nyoe, "Has the sparrow the Buddha-Nature or not?"
Nyoe answered, "Yes!"
Saigun said, "Then why does it make droppings on the head of Buddha?"
Nyoe replied, "Does it make droppings on the head of a hawk?"

(That is to say, it is not devoid of discrimination as you suggest, and its Buddha nature manifests itself here, in this very acting according to circumstances.)

~ Mumonkan (Originally titled 'Zen and Zen Classics, Vol. 4'), Translated by R.H. Blyth [Commentary on Case 1] ~

HOW TO RUB MY EYES?

There was a young monk whose name was Tan-yuan. Once, after returning from a pilgrimage, he went to the Patriarch Ma-Tsu and drew a circle in front of him. He then entered the circle, bowed, and stood still. The Patriarch asked him, "Is it that you want to become a Buddha?"

The young monk replied, "I do not know how to rub my eyes."

The Patriarch said, "I am not as good as you."

The young monk had no answer.

~ Sun Face Buddha ~

GO BACK

When Ch'an Master Hui-lang went to see the Patriarch Ma-Tsu for the first time, the Patriarch asked him, "What are you seeking by coming here?"

Hui-lang replied, "I am seeking for the Buddha's knowledge and insight."

The Patriarch said, "The Buddha has no knowledge and insight; knowledge and insight belong to Mara. Where are you coming from?"

Hui-lang replied, "I am coming from Nan-yueh."

The Patriarch said, "You are coming from Nan-yueh, and yet do not know the essence of the mind of Ts'ao- hsi. You should return there quickly. You need not go to other places."

(Ts'ao-hsi is the name of the place where the monastery of the Sixth Patriarch is located. So, the phrase "the mind of Ts'ao hsi" means the mind of the Sixth Patriarch, or simply the enlightened mind.)

~ Sun-Face Buddha ~

ANY FAULT?

Once the Zen Master Nan-chuan said, "Ma-tsu taught that mind is Buddha. Elder Master Wang (means Nan-chuan himself) does not say it that way. It is not mind, it is not Buddha, it is not a thing: is there still any fault in this statement?"

Chaochou bowed and left. One of the monks followed Chao-chou, and asked him, "What did the Venerable mean by bowing and then going out?"

Chaochou said, "You can go and ask the Abbot."

The monk went back to Nan-chuan, and asked, "What did Venerable Shen (Chaochou) mean [by acting in that way]?"

The Master said, "He understood my meaning."

~ Adapted from Case 57 of "Every End Exposed: The 100 Koans of Master Kido - With the Answers of Hakuin - Zen" ~

BASO'S "THIS VERY MIND IS THE BUDDHA"

Daibai asked Baso, "What is the Buddha?"

Baso answered, "This very mind is the Buddha."

~ Mumonkan, The Gateless Gate, by Ekai, called Mu-mon, tr. Nyogen Senzaki and Paul Reps ~

KILL THE BUDDHA

When Buddha was born, he took seven steps, looked in the four directions, pointed with one hand to the sky and with the other hand to the ground, and said, "I alone am the honored one above and below Heaven."

Somebody once mentioned these words of the baby Buddha to Zen Master Yunmen and asked what they meant. Yunmen said, "If I had seen what he did at that time, I would have killed him with a single blow and given him to a dog to eat up. And I would thus attempt to bring great peace to all under Heaven."

~ (Collected Works of Korean Buddhism, Volume 7-1) Gongan Collections I Edited and Translated by John Jorgensen ~

THE CARDINAL PRINCIPLE

When Elder Ding came to see Linji he asked, "What is the cardinal principle of the Buddhadharma?"

The master got down from his rope-bottomed chair. Seizing Ding, he gave him a slap and pushed him away. Ding stood still.

A monk standing by said, "Elder Ding, why don't you bow?" Just as he bowed, Ding attained great enlightenment.

~The Record of Rinzai ~

THE GREAT CROSSING

The Buddha said: "A man beginning a long journey sees ahead a vast body of water. There is neither boat nor bridge. To escape the dangers of his present location, he constructs a raft of grass and branches. When he reaches the other side, he realizes how useful the raft was and wonders if he should hoist it on his back and carry it with him forever. Now if he did this, would he be wise? Or, having crossed to safety, should he place the raft in a high dry location for someone else to use? This is the way I have taught the dharma, the doctrine - for crossing, not for keeping. Cast aside every proper state of mind, oh monks - much less wrong ones - and remember well to leave the raft behind!"

~ Alagaddupama Sutta ~

AN INSOLENT WAYFARER

In ancient times it was customary for a traveling monk seeking lodging at a Zen monastery to engage in dharma combat with the abbot or head monk. If the wayfarer won the debate, he could stay; if not, he had to seek quarters elsewhere.

Once a master assigned his attendant to engage in such an encounter with a traveling monk, who challenged him to a silent debate. It so happened that this attendant had but one eye.

Soon the wayfarer returned to the master, saying, "Your man is too good for me. I must journey on. I held up one finger to symbolize the Buddha. But he held up two fingers for the Buddha and the Dharma. So, I held up three fingers for the Buddha, the Dharma and the Sangha. But then he held up a clenched fist to indicate they were all one - so I ran to indicate I am no match for him."

When the traveller who spoke these words left, the attendant arrived - angry and out of breath. "Where is that rascal?" he demanded. "First, he insulted me by holding up one finger to indicate I had only one eye. Determined to be polite in spite of that, I held up two fingers to indicate that, on the other hand, he was blessed with two eyes. But he just kept rubbing it in, for next he held up three fingers to indicate that all together there were only three eyes among us. So, I went to hit him and he ran off! Where is he hiding?"

~ Source: Unknown ~

THE MEANING

A monk asked, "Putting aside 'Mind is Buddha,' what is the meaning of 'No mind, no Buddha'?"

Taiping said, "Yesterday a monk asked me this. I didn't answer him."

The monk said, "I don't understand whether this is much different from 'Mind is Buddha.'"

Taiping said, "It's as close as ten thousand miles away. It's as far as a gap that a hair can't fit into."

~ Zen's Chinese Heritage by Andy Ferguson ~

UNDERSTANDING THE DHARMA

A monk once asked Zen Master Hui-Neng (The sixth patriarch of Zen)," Who has attained the essential principle of Huangmei (The Fifth Ancestor, the master of Hui-Neng)?"

Hui-neng said, "Those who understand the Buddhadharma."

The monk said, "Has the master attained it?"

Hui-neng said, "I haven't attained it."

The monk said, "Why haven't you attained it?"

Hui-neng said, "Because I don't understand the Buddhadharma."

~ Dogen's 300 Koans ~

THE GREAT MEANING

Daowu asked, "What is the great meaning of the Buddhadharma?"

Shitou said, "Not attaining. Not knowing."

Daowu asked, "Is there anything beyond this?"

Shitou said, "The sky does not obstruct the white cloud's flight."

~ Zen's Chinese Heritage by Andy Ferguson ~

WHERE DID YOU COME FROM?

Zen Master Qingyuan, upon Shitou's arrival: "Where did you come from?"

Shitou: "I came from Tsaohsi," (He came from the Sixth Patriarch.)

Qingyuan: "Did you attain anything there?"

Shitou: "I was not missing anything even before I got there," (As his Buddha-nature was complete even before he went there, there was nothing to attain.)

Qingyuan: "If you are not in need of anything, why did you go to Tsaohsi?"

Shitou: "If I had not gone to Tsaohsi, how would I know that I was not in need of anything?" (If he had not gone to Tsaohsi, he would not have realized that he always had the Buddha-nature.)

~http://poetrychina.net/Story_of_Zen/zenstory13.htm~

THE SUTRAS

Someone asked, "If we interpret in accordance with the sutras, the Buddhas of the Three Worlds hate sutras, every word, as though they were the chatter of demons. What about this?"

Zen Master Po-chang [Baizhang Huaihai (720-814)] said "If we hang on tight to circumstances the Buddhas of the Three Worlds hate it; if we seek anywhere else outside this, it's the chatter of demons."

~ Record of the life of the Ch'an master Po-chang Huai-hai [Bojang Whyhigh] Translated by Gary Snyder ~

WIFE AND CHILDREN

After Zhizang became abbot of the Western Hall [in Chinese, Xitang], a lay-person asked him, "Is there a heaven and hell?"

Zhizang said, "There is."

The layman then asked, "Is there really a Buddha, Dharma and Sangha - the three jewels?"

Zhizang said, "There are."

The layman then asked several other questions, and to each Zhizang answered, "There are."

The layman said, "Is the master sure there's no mistake about this?"

Zhizang said, "When you visited other teachers, what did they say?"

The layman said, "I once visited Master Jingshan."

Zhizang said, "What did Jingshan say to you?"

The layman said, "He said that there wasn't a single thing."

Zhizang said, "Do you have a wife and children?"

The layman said, "Yes."

Zhizang said, "Does Master Jingshan have a wife and children?"

The layman said, "No."

Zhizang said, "Then it's okay for Jingshan to say there isn't a single thing."

The layman bowed, thanked Zhizang, and then went away.

[Master Hsing Yun has explained:

Zhizang meant, "Do you see? When Jingshan answered 'no' to your questions, he was speaking from his own enlightened point of view. When I answered 'yes,' I was speaking from your worldly point of view."]

~ Zen's Chinese Heritage by Andy Ferguson ~

OPEN YOUR OWN TREASURE HOUSE

Daju visited the Zen master Ma-Tzu (Mazu or Baso) in China.

Mazu asked, "From where have you come?"

Daju said, "From Yue Province."

Mazu then asked, "What were you planning to do by coming here?"

Daju said, "I've come to seek the Buddhadharma (i.e., the way of awakening)."

Mazu then replied, "I don't have anything here, so what 'Buddhadharma' do you think you're going to find here? You haven't seen the treasure in your own house, so why have you run off to some other place?"

Daju then said, "Where is my treasure house?"

Mazu then said, "It is just who is asking me this question, that is your treasury. It is replete, not lacking in the slightest, and if you realize its embodiment then why would you go seeking it elsewhere?"

Upon hearing these words, Daju perceived his fundamental mind unobstructed by thinking. He ardently thanked and honored Mazu for this instruction. Ever after he urged his friends: "Open your own treasure house and use those treasures."

~ Zen's Chinese Heritage by Andy Ferguson ~

THE TRUE BODY

An inquirer asked Yanguan Qian, "Who was the Buddha?"

Yanguan replied by requesting of his visitor, "Would you please pass me that water-pitcher."

The inquirer looked around, saw the pitcher, and passed it to the master. Yanguan poured himself a cup of water and then asked the visitor to replace the pitcher. The visitor did so, then, thinking that perhaps Yanguan had not heard his original question, put it again: "About the Buddha—who was he?"

"Oh, yes," Yanguan said. "Well, you know, he's been dead a long time now."

~ Zen Masters of China by Richard Bryan McDaniel ~

EXPOSED

Someone asked, "If one kills one's father and mother, one can repent in front of the Buddha. Where does one repent if one kills the Buddha and the patriarchs?"
Zen Master Yunmen said, "Exposed!"

~ Records of Yunmen ~

I killed my parents.
I now repent to Buddha.
If I killed Buddha,
Where will I repent?

(Perfectly clear.)

~ Zen Master Seung Sahn ~
~ Source: Teaching Letters of Zen Master Seung Sahn ~

THE WAY OF AWAKENING

There was a monk who asked his master, "What did Bodhidharma bring when he came from the West?"

Zen Master Yaoshan replied, "He didn't bring anything."

The monk insisted, "Didn't Bodhidharma bring Buddhadharma, the teaching of Buddha, from the West?"

The master replied, "No, not really. Buddhadharma has always been in China."

The monk was puzzled, "Well, that's strange then. If Buddhadharma was already here, why did Bodhidharma bother coming to China?"

The master replied, "Because Buddhadharma was already here, it is for that reason that Bodhidharma had to leave India and come here."

~ Zen's Chinese Heritage by Andy Ferguson ~

THE OTHER BUDDHA

The monk Zun, who was serving as altar attendant in Yaoshan's community, was washing Buddha statues. The master came by and said, "I see you've washed this one; can you wash the other Buddha, too?"

Zun said, "Please hand me the other Buddha."

The master stopped questioning.

~ Zen's Chinese Heritage by Andy Ferguson ~

DANXIA BURNS A BUDDHA IMAGE

Once when Zen master Danxia Tianran was staying at the temple Huilin si in the capital on a very cold day he took a wooden buddha image from the buddha hall, set it on fire, and warmed himself by the flames.

The temple supervisor happened to see this and scolded Danxia, saying, "How can you burn my wooden buddha!"

Danxia stirred the ashes with his staff and said, "I'm burning it to get the holy relics."1

The supervisor replied, "How could there be relics in a wooden buddha?"

"If there are no relics," Danxia answered, "then please give me the two attendant images to burn."

~ Entangling Vines: A Classic Collection of Zen Koans by Thomas Yuho Kirchner~

A ZEN DIALOGUE

A monk asked, "How does one speak of the great mystery?"
Zen Master Daowu said, "Don't say 'I have realized the Buddhadharma!'"
The monk asked, "How do you deal with students who are stuck?"
Daowu said, "Why don't you ask me?"
The monk said, "I just asked you."
Daowu said, "Go! This isn't the place where you'll find relief."

~ Zen's Chinese Heritage by Andy Ferguson ~

WHO IS THE TEACHER OF ALL BUDDHAS?

A monk asked, "What is the great way?"
Zen Master Changsha Jingcen said, "It doesn't exclude you."
The monk asked, "Who is the teacher of all buddhas?"
Changsha said, "For the incalculable eon, who has ever concealed this?"

~ Zen's Chinese Heritage by Andy Ferguson ~

BUDDHA IS AFFLICTION

Zen Master Joshu entered the hall and addressed the monks, saying "Buddha is affliction. Affliction is Buddha."
A monk said, "I don't understand whose house is afflicted by Buddha."
Joshu said, "All people are afflicted by Buddha."
The monk asked, "How can affliction be avoided?"
Joshu said, "Why avoid it?"

~ Zen's Chinese Heritage by Andy Ferguson ~

THE GENUINE BUDDHA

Zen Master Joshu entered the hall and addressed the monks, saying, "A metal buddha does not withstand the furnace. A wooden Buddha does not withstand the fire. A mud Buddha does not withstand water. The genuine Buddha sits within you......
".. Try sitting in Zazen for twenty or thirty years, and if you still don't understand then cut off my head! "

~ Zen's Chinese Heritage by Andy Ferguson ~

WHEN?

A monk asked, "Does the cypress tree in the garden have Buddha nature or not?"
Zen Master Joshu said, "It has."
The monk asked, "When will it become a buddha?"
Joshu said, "When the sky falls to earth."
The monk asked, "When will the sky fall to earth?"
Joshu said, "When the cypress becomes a Buddha."

~ Various Ancient Records; See Bibliography ~

THE TEACHING

Cuiwei asked Zen master Danxia, "What is the teaching of all buddhas?"
Danxia exclaimed, "Fortunately, life is fundamentally wonderful. Why do you need to take up a cleaning cloth and broom?"
Wuxue retreated three steps.
Danxia said, "Wrong."
Wuxue again came forward.
Danxia said, "Wrong. Wrong."
Wuxue then lifted one foot into the air, spun in a circle and went out.
Danxia said, "Such an answer! It's turning one's back on all the buddhas."
Upon hearing these words, Wuxue attained great enlightenment.
Later, when Wuxue was abbot of a temple, Touzi Yiqing said to him, "I'm not clear about what resulted when the Second Ancestor first saw Bodhidharma."
Zen master Wuxue said, "Right now you can see me. What is the result?"
At that moment Touzi suddenly awakened to the profound mystery.

~ Zen's Chinese Heritage by Andy Ferguson ~

THE GREAT MEANING

Zen master Muzhou asked a monk, "Where do you come from?"

The monk said, "From Liuyang."

Muzhou said, "What does the teacher there say when a student asks him about the great meaning of the Buddhadharma?"

The monk said, "He says, 'Traveling everywhere without a path.'"

Muzhou said, "Does that teacher really say that or not?"

The monk said, "He really does say that."

Muzhou took his staff and struck the monk, saying, "This fool just repeats words!"

~ Zen's Chinese Heritage by Andy Ferguson ~

THERE IS NO BUDDHA

Zen master Rinzai once said:
"Friends I tell you this: there is no Buddha, no spiritual path to follow, no training and no realization. What are you feverishly running after? Putting a head on top of your own head, you blind idiots! Your head is right where it should be. The trouble lies in your not believing in yourselves enough. Because you don't believe in yourselves you are knocked here and there by all the conditions in which you find yourselves. Being enslaved and turned around by objective situations, you have no freedom whatever, you are not masters of yourselves. Stop turning to the outside and don't be attached to my words either. Just cease clinging to the past and hankering after the future."

~ The Record of Rinzai ~

THE ESSENTIAL MEANING

Huileng of Changqing studied with Lingyun and asked him, "What is the essential meaning of Buddhadharma?"

Lingyun said, "When the donkey matter has not yet left, the horse matter arrives."

~ Zen's Chinese Heritage by Andy Ferguson ~

DON'T STUDY THE WORDS OF BUDDHAS

One day Zen master Jiashan entered the hall and addressed the monks, saying, "Since the times of the ancestors there have been those who misunderstand what has been passed down. Right up to now they have used the words of the Buddhas and ancestors and made them models for study. If people do this, then they'll go crazy and have no wisdom at all. The Buddhas and ancestors have instructed you that the dharma-less root is the Way. The Way is without even a single Dharma. There is no Buddha that you can become. There is no way that can be attained. Nor is there any Dharma that can be grasped or let go of. Therefore, the ancients said, 'Before the eyes there is no Dharma, but the meaning is before the eyes.' Those who want to study the Buddhas and ancestors haven't opened their eyes. Why do they want to submit to something else and not attain their own freedom? Basically, it's because they are confused about life and death. They realize they don't have a bit of freedom, so they go thousands of miles to seek out some great teacher. Those people must attain the true eye, not spend their time grasping and discarding spurious views. But are there any here among you of definite attainment who can really hold forth about existence and nonexistence? If there's someone who's definite about this then I invite you to speak out.

"When persons of high ability hear these words, they are clear about what's being said. Those of middle or low ability continue rushing around. Why don't you just directly face life and death? Don't tell me you still want the Buddhas and ancestors to live and die in your place! People who understand will laugh at you.

"If you still don't get it, then listen to this verse:

Belabouring life and death,
Just seeking Buddha's quarter,
Confused about the truth before your eyes,
Poking a fire to find a cool spot."

~ Zen's Chinese Heritage by Andy Ferguson ~

SOUND OF BUDDHA

A monk asked, "All sounds are the sound of Buddha, are they not?"
Zen Master Touzi said, "Yes."
The monk said, "Does the master not make farting sounds on the commode?"
Touzi struck the monk.

~ Zen's Chinese Heritage by Andy Ferguson ~

GET OUT!

Once a monk asked Zen Master Deshan Xuanjian, "What is awakening?"
Deshan struck him with his staff and said, "Get out, don't defecate here!"
Then the monk asked, "What is Buddha?"
The master said, "An old beggar in India."

~ Zen's Chinese Heritage by Andy Ferguson ~

HUANGBO BOWS TO A BUDDHA IMAGE

One day, when Zen Master Huangbo was bowing before a Buddha image in the Buddha Hall, the novice Xuan asked, "If we should 'seek nothing from the Buddha, seek nothing from the Dharma, and seek nothing from the Sangha,' then what does your venerable seek by bowing to the Buddha?" Master Huangbo replied, "Seeking nothing from the Buddha, seeking nothing from the Dharma, seeking nothing from the Sangha - that's how I always do prostrations."
"Why bow then?" Xuan insisted.
Master Huangbo slapped the novice.
"How rude!" Xuan said.
"What sort of place is this to be talking about rudeness or courtesy?" Master replied and he slapped Xuan again.

~Entangling Vines: A Classic Collection of Zen Koans by Thomas Yuho Kirchner~

THE SECRET

Fenzhou Wuye (760-821) was a native of Shangluo in Shangzhou, in present-day Shanxi. From the age of nine he studied the Mahayana sutras at Kaiyuan si. It was said that he could memorize the texts, five lines at a time, at a single reading. He received ordination at the age of twelve and the full precepts at the age of twenty. He was well versed in the vinaya and often lectured on the Mahāparinirvāṇa Sūtra.
Hearing of Zen Master Mazu Daoyi, Wuye went to visit him. The master, noting Wuye's imposing appearance and voice, remarked, "An impressive buddha hall, but no buddha inside."
Wuye knelt down and said, "I have studied and understood the teachings of the Three Vehicles, but I have not yet understood the Zen teaching that mind, just as it is, is Buddha."
Mazu replied, "It is the very mind that has not yet understood - there is nothing else."
Wuye questioned further, "What is the secretly transmitted mind-seal that the Patriarch brought from the West?"
Mazu replied, "Virtuous monk, you're becoming annoying; go now and come again some other time."
As Wuye stepped out Mazu called, "Virtuous monk!"
When Wuye looked around Mazu said, "What is that!"

Wuye understood and bowed to Mazu. Mazu said, "This stupid oaf (fellow)! What's all this bowing about?"

~ Zen's Chinese Heritage by Andy Ferguson ~

THE DECEPTIVE BUDDHA

Zen master Longya once entered the hall and addressed the monks, saying, 'Those people who penetrate the study must pass beyond Buddhas and Patriarchs.' The Master of Xinfeng said, 'The buddhas and ancestors are like deceptive thieves. If you see the verbal teachings of the Buddhas and Patriarchs as if they were your mortal enemies, only then will you have the qualifications for penetrating the study. If you can't pass beyond them, then you will be deceived by the Patriarchs and Buddhas.'

At the time, there was a monk who asked, 'Do the Patriarchs and Buddhas have any intention to deceive people or not?'
Longya said, 'Tell me, do rivers and lakes have any intention to obstruct people or not?' He went on to say, 'Although rivers and lakes have no intention to obstruct people, it's just that people now can't cross them. Therefore, rivers and lakes after all become barriers to people. You cannot say that rivers and lakes do not obstruct people.

Although the Patriarchs and Buddhas have no intention to deceive people, it's just that people now cannot pass beyond them. So, Patriarchs and Buddhas after all deceive people. Again, you cannot say that Patriarchs and Buddhas do not deceive people. If one can pass beyond the Patriarchs and Buddhas, this person surpasses the Patriarchs and Buddhas.

Still, one must completely realize the intent of the Patriarchs and Buddhas: only then can one be equal to those transcendent people of old. If you have not yet been able to pass through, if you study the Buddhas and study the Patriarchs, then you'll have no hope of attaining even in ten thousand eons.'
The monk also asked 'How can I be able to avoid being deceived by the Patriarchs and Buddhas?' Longya said, 'You must be enlightened yourself.'

~ Zen's Chinese Heritage by Andy Ferguson ~

I ASK YOU

A monk asked, "What is the talk that is beyond the Buddhas and ancestors?"
Zen master Qianfeng said, "I ask you."
The monk said, "Master, please don't ask me."
Qianfeng said, "If I ask you, it doesn't make any difference. So, I ask you, what is the talk that is beyond the Buddhas and ancestors?"

~ Zen's Chinese Heritage by Andy Ferguson ~

LIFE AND DEATH

As the monks Jiashan and Dingshan were travelling together they had a discussion. Dingshan said, "When there is no Buddha within life and death, then there is no life and death." Jiashan said, "When Buddha is within life and death, there is no confusion about life and death." The two monks couldn't reach any agreement, so they climbed the mountain to see Zen master Damei Fachang (who used to live on Mount Da Mei).
Jiashan raised their question with Damei and asked, "We'd like to know which viewpoint is most intimate?"
Damei said, "Go now. Come back tomorrow."
The next day Jiashan again came to Damei and raised the question of the previous day.
Damei said, "The one who's intimate doesn't ask. The one asks isn't intimate." (Years later, when Jiashan was abbot, he said, "At that time I lost my eye.")

~ Zen's Chinese Heritage by Andy Ferguson ~

WHO ARE BUDDHAS?

A monk asked Zen Master Luzu Baoyun of Chizhou, "Who are all the Buddhas and saints?"
Baoyun said, "Not the ones with crowns on their heads."
The monk said, "Then who are they?"
Baoyun said, "The ones without crowns."

~ Zen's Chinese Heritage by Andy Ferguson ~

DO YOU UNDERSTAND?

A monk asked, "Fundamentally, can people become Buddhas or not?"
Zen master Changhsa said, "Do you think that the emperor of the Great Tang still plows a field and harvests the rice?"
The monk said, "I still don't understand who it is who becomes a Buddha."
Changsha said, "It's you that becomes a Buddha."
The monk was silent.
Changsha said,"Do you understand?"
The monk said, "No."
Changsha said," If someone trips on the ground and falls down, and then they use the ground to get up again - does the ground say anything?"

~ Zen's Chinese Heritage by Andy Ferguson ~

THE ESSENTIAL MEANING

A monk asked Zen Master Joshu, "What is the essential meaning of the Buddhadharma?" Joshu said, "The cypress tree at the front of the courtyard."

~ Zen's Chinese Heritage by Andy Ferguson. This is also Case 9 of Entangling Vines, Case 119 of Dogen's 300 Koans and Case 47 of Shoyoroku ~

THE WHISK

A monk asked, "What is the essential Dharma of all the Buddhas?"
Zen Master Dasui held up his whisk and said, "Do you understand?"
The monk said, "No."
Dasui said, "A whisk."

~ Zen's Chinese Heritage by Andy Ferguson ~

SONG OF ENLIGHTENMENT

Do you not see him, the really wise man,
always at ease, unmoved?

He does not get rid of illusion,
nor does he seek for the truth.

Ignorance is intrinsically the Buddha nature,
our illusory unreal body is the cosmic body.

Getting rid of things
and clinging to emptiness
is an illness of the same kind;

It is just like throwing oneself into a fire
to avoid being drowned.

~ Zen Master Yongjia Xuanjue (665-713) ~

BUDDHA, A CLUMP OF DIRT

After Yanyang assumed the abbacy of a temple, a monk asked him, "What is Buddha?"
Yanyang said, "A clump of dirt."
The monk asked, "What is Dharma?"
Yanyang said, "The ground is moving."
The monk asked, "What is Sangha?"
Yanyang said, "Eating porridge and rice."

~ Zen's Chinese Heritage by Andy Ferguson ~

DONKEY

When Nanta returned to Zen Master Yangshan, Yangshan said, "Why have you come?"
Nanta said, "To pay respects to the master."
Yangshan said, "Do you still see me?"
Nanta said, "Yes."
Yangshan said, "Do I look like a donkey?"
Nanta said, "When I observe the master, you don't look like a Buddha."
Yangshan said, "If I don't look like a Buddha, then what do I look like?"
Nanta said, "If I must compare you to something, then how do you differ from a donkey?"
Yangshan cried out excitedly, "He's forgotten both ordinary and sacred! The passions are exhausted and the body is revealed. For twenty years I've tested them in this way and no one has gotten it. Now this disciple has done it!"
Yangshan would always point to Nanta and say to people, "This disciple is a living Buddha."

~ Zen's Chinese Heritage by Andy Ferguson ~

BLIND, DEAF AND MUTE

Zen Master Xuansha gave instruction to the congregation, saying: "The great masters everywhere speak extensively of reaching and benefiting beings. If they encountered three persons with different disabilities, how would they reach them? For a blind person, if they wielded the staff or raised their whisk then the person would not see it. For a deaf person, if they spoke of samadhi, then he would not hear it. For a mute person, if they called on him to speak, he could not do so. So, what would they do to reach them? If these types cannot be reached, then the Buddhadharma has no effect."

~ Zen's Chinese Heritage by Andy Ferguson ~

HEY YOU

Once Xuansha said, "All of you practitioners of Zen, you've traveled here from every quarter on foot, asking me to help you practice Zen and study Tao. You've taken this place to be special, and when you get here you ask every sort of question. Since this is what you've done, then you should check this place out thoroughly! Haven't I been completely forthcoming with you? I extinguish what you know. Then what is there left? If nothing is left, then of what use is your knowledge? Since you've come here, I now ask you, do any of you have the eye of wisdom or not? If so, then let us see it now. Can we see it? If not, then I call you all blind and deaf. Is that it? Are you willing to speak up in this manner? Virtuous Zennists do not willingly submit. Are you authentic monks? The top of your head is exposed to all Buddhas in the ten directions. You don't dare show the slightest error!"

~ Zen's Chinese Heritage by Andy Ferguson ~

CLARITY

A monk asked, "What is the mind of all Buddhas?"
Xianglin said, "Clarity. From beginning to end, clarity."
A monk asked, "How can I understand this?"
Xianglin said, "Don't be deceived by others."

~ Zen's Chinese Heritage by Andy Ferguson ~

THE ANCIENT BUDDHAS

A monk asked, "What was the style of the ancient Buddhas?"
Zen Master Fayan Wenyi said, "Where can it not be completely seen?"

~ Zen's Chinese Heritage by Andy Ferguson ~

UNDERSTANDING

A monk asked, "What is Buddha?"
Zen Master Chongshou said, "What is Buddha?"
The monk asked, "What is understanding?"
Chongshou said, "Understanding is not understanding."

~ Zen's Chinese Heritage by Andy Ferguson ~

THE LAST POEM

When Zen Master Touzi Yiqing was near death, he composed a poem:

As the abbot of two temples,
I couldn't assist the Buddha way.
My parting message to you all,
Don't go seeking after something.

Touzi then put down the brush and passed away.

~ Zen's Chinese Heritage by Andy Ferguson ~

LOOK AND LISTEN

A monk asked, "Our tradition has the saying, 'All the Buddhas and their teachings come forth from this scripture.' What is 'this scripture'?"
Zen Master Yongming said, "Without intention or sound it is endlessly recited."
The monk asked, "How does one receive and uphold it?"
Yongming said, "Those who want to receive and uphold it must look and listen."

~ Zen's Chinese Heritage by Andy Ferguson ~

HELP!

Zen master Furong Daokai addressed the monks, saying, "I don't ask about the last thirty days of the twelfth month. I just want to know about the great matter of the twelfth month. Everyone! At that moment, Buddha can't help you, Dharma can't help you, the ancestors can't help you, all the teachers on earth can't help you, I can't help you, and the King of Death can't help you. You must settle this matter now! If you settle it now, the Buddha can't take it from you, the Dharma can't take it from you, the ancestors can't take it from you, all the teachers in the world, and the King of Death can't take it from you.
"Speak out! What is the lesson of this very moment? Do you understand? Next year there'll be a new shoot growing. The annoying spring wind never ceases."

~ Zen's Chinese Heritage by Andy Ferguson ~

REFLECTION

While spending the summer at Mt. Gui, Baofeng heard the story of a monk who asked Zen Master Yunmen, "Isn't the Buddhadharma like the moon reflected in water?"
Yunmen said, "The clear wave does not penetrate the Way."
Baofeng, hearing this story, gained a great insight.

~ Zen's Chinese Heritage by Andy Ferguson ~

THE STRANGE LECTURE

Zen master Yunan Kewen said to the congregation, "Everyone! Has your self-belief gone far enough? If you've reached the zenith of belief in self, then you know that self-nature is fundamentally Buddha. When you thus realize no belief in self, then you've become a Buddha. But because of ancient delusion, when a person hears this, it's difficult for him to forsake his belief [in self]. The speech and words of the virtuous, from ancient times down to the present, throughout the current of Zen, have been nothing but the Buddha nature of the saints flowing out and being set forth. But what flowed forth was just the branch. Buddha nature is the root.
"These days many people seek the branch but reject the root, forgetting the true and falling into false, they have harmed the Buddhadharma. What an annoyance it is for them that they should remember that the words and phrases of the ancients were for the sake of Zen and the Way! If not for Bodhidharma's coming from the west, there'd be no Zen to be passed on. It was all for the sake of beings to individually realize their own self-nature and become Buddhas, for beings to personally bring forth the entire Buddhadharma. Moreover, it was for the transformation of the universal spirit, whereby all beings are seen to be, in themselves, complete and perfect, and without

the need to falsely seek anything outside of themselves.

"If people today seek something outside of themselves, then they cover up the root and will never gain awakening. If one always acts as guest, whereby the countless treasures belong to others, then it is just delusive thinking, and ultimately the flowing cycle of birth and death can't be avoided."

~ Zen's Chinese Heritage by Andy Ferguson ~

THE ATTENDANT

Zen master Baoning Renyong entered the hall to address the monks. The attendant lit incense [to present to the Buddha].

Baoning pointed to the attendant and said, "The attendant has already expounded the Dharma for all of you!"

~ Zen's Chinese Heritage by Andy Ferguson ~

THE SUPPORT

[An old Indian-Chinese Buddhist tradition holds that someone who makes false statements concerning the Dharma, the spiritual Way or Truth, will lose all his facial hairs.] Zen Master Baoing said, "If you say that the Buddhadharma supports all beings, you won't avoid having your eyebrows fall out. If you say that the worldly dharmas support all beings, you shoot straight into hell like an arrow.
"But aside from these two ways of speaking, what can I say today? There's no use for the three-inch tongue. The two empty hands can't make a fist!"

~ Source: Unknown ~

COMPLETE AWAKENING

Zen Master Baofeng entered the hall and addressed the monks, saying, "An ancient Buddhas said, 'When I first gained complete awakening, I personally saw that all beings of the great earth are each fully endowed with complete and perfect enlightenment.' And later he said, 'It's a great mystery. No one can fathom it.' I don't see anyone who understands this. Just some blowhards." He then got down from the seat.

~ Zen's Chinese Heritage by Andy Ferguson ~

THE BUDDHAS

Zen Master Baofeng entered the hall and addressed the monks, saying, "All the Buddhas of bygone ages have already entered nirvana. You people! Don't be nostalgic about them. The Buddhas of the future have not yet appeared in the world. All of you, don't be deluded! On this very day who are you? Study this!"

~ Zen's Chinese Heritage by Andy Ferguson ~

THE ORDER

The World Honored One (The Buddha), without having yet departed Tusita, had already descended into the palace and, without having yet left his mother's womb, had already completed the task of saving people.

~ The First Case of 'Korean Gongan Collection' ~

CRYING BABIES

Zen Master Hongzhi Zhengue (1091-1157) addressed the monks, saying, "When the Buddhas talk about Dharma, they're just using yellow leaves to stop babies from crying. When the ancestors transmit the teaching, they're just making empty-handed threats. When you reach this point, you must [attain] self-cessation, self-realization, and self-clarity. The Buddha is realized in each individual person, and the Dharma can't be passed to you by someone else. If you understand in this manner, then you are a great adept, a true patch-robed monk, and you have successfully completed the great affair.
"Brethren! How, after all, will you finally find peace? Just wait for the snow to melt and naturally spring will arrive."

~ Zen's Chinese Heritage by Andy Ferguson ~

AS THE BUDDHAS SAW

Daio said to Genchu: Since ancient times, the enlightened ancestors appearing in the world relied just on their own fundamental experience to reveal something of what is before us: so, we see them knocking chairs and raising whisks, hitting the ground and brandishing sticks, beating a drum or rolling balls...

Daio continued: Even though this is so, eminent Genchu, you have travelled all over and spent a long time in monasteries. Don't worry about such old calendar days as these I mentioned -- just go by the living road you see on your own; going east, going west, like a hawk sailing through the skies. In the blink of an eye you cross over to the other side.

On another occasion Daio said to Kusho: The cause and conditions of the one great concern of the enlightened ones is not apart from your daily affairs. There is no difference between here and there. It pervades past and present, shining through the heavens, mirroring the earth. That is why it is said that everything in the last myriad eons is right in the present. We value the great spirit of a hero only in those concerned. Before any signs become distinct, before any illustration is evident, concentrate fiercely, looking, looking, coming or going, till your effort is completely ripe. In the moment of a thought, you attain union. The mind of birth and death is destroyed and suddenly you clearly see your original appearance, the scene of your native land; each particular distinctly clear. You then see and hear just as the Buddhas did, know and act as the enlightened ancestors did.

~ The Buddha: The Emptiness of The Heart by Osho ~

INSUFFICIENT

Yuanwu Keqin (1063-1135) was a gifted person who thoroughly studied the Confucian classics and other Buddhist scriptures. Once he became deathly ill. He realized that his scriptural study and chanting of Buddha's name was insufficient, saying, "The true path of nirvana of all the Buddhas is not found in words. I've used sounds to seek form, but it's of no use for dealing with death." After he recovered, he set off to seek instruction from the Zen school.
Later on, he got enlightened and became a famous Zen Master.

~Adapted from Zen's Chinese Heritage by Andy Ferguson ~

THE MEANING

A monk asked Yangshan [Huiji], "What is the meaning of the Patriarch's coming from the West?" Yangshan drew a circle in the air with a finger, and wrote a Chinese character of "Buddha" inside the circle. The monk was in silence.

~ The Record of Transmission of the Lamp, Book 11
~

ZEN

Zen Master Yuanwu Keqin (1063-1135) entered the hall and said, "Zen is without thought or intention. Setting forth a single intention goes against the essential doctrine. The great Way ends all meritorious work. When merit is established, the essential principle is lost. Upon hearing a clear sound or some external words, do not seek some meaning within them. Rather, turn the light inward and use the essential function to pound off the manacles of the Buddhas and ancestors. Where Buddha is, there is also guest and host. Where there is no Buddha, the wind roars across the earth. But when the mind's intentions are stilled, even a great noise becomes a soothing sound. Tell me, where can such a person be found? Put on a shawl and stand outside the thousand peaks. Draw water and pour it on the plants before the five stars."

~ Zen's Chinese Heritage by Andy Ferguson ~

THE BUDDHA

When Hyakujo was a young boy, his mother took him to a temple, and entering, she bowed to the Buddhist statue.
Pointing to the statue, Hyakujo asked his mother, "What's that?"
"That's a Buddha," she replied.
Hyakujo said, "He looks like a man. I want to become a Buddha afterwards."
Many years later, Hyakujo became a monk. One day, as attendant to Baso, he went wandering in the mountains. On his return he suddenly began to weep.
One of his fellow monks said, "Are you thinking of your father and mother?"
"No," said Hyakujo.
"Did somebody slander you?" asked the monk.
"No," answered Hyakujo.
"Then what are you weeping for?" persisted the monk.
"Go and ask the master," said Hyakujo.
The monk went and asked Baso, who said, "Go and ask Hyakujo."
The monk came back to the room and found Hyakujo laughing.
"You were weeping a little while ago; why are you laughing now?" he asked.
Hyakujo said, "I was weeping a little while ago, and now I am laughing."

~ Zen: The Quantum Leap from Mind to No Mind by Osho ~

ENLIGHTENMENT WITHIN DELUSION

Huguo Jingyuan (1094-1146) was a disciple of Zen Master Yuanwu Keqin. Once Jingyuan overheard a monk reading a teaching by Zen Master Sixin that said, "Because enlightenment is realized in delusion, in enlightenment one recognizes the delusion within enlightenment and the enlightenment within delusion. When enlightenment and delusion are both forgotten, then one may establish all dharmas from this place that is without enlightenment and delusion." When Jingyuan heard this, he experienced doubt. But later, when he was hurrying to the Buddha hall, just as he pushed open the door, he suddenly experienced vast enlightenment.

~ Zen's Chinese Heritage by Andy Ferguson ~

KILL THE BUDDHA

One day Zen master Huguo Jingyuan (1094-1146) entered the hall and addressed the monks, saying, "When the old Shakyamuni was born, he was really a laughingstock. With one hand he pointed at the sky and with the other he pointed at the earth, and then he said, 'I alone am the honored one.' Later, the great teacher Yunmen said: 'If I had been there and seen that, then for the sake of peace in the world I would have beaten him to death and fed him to the dogs'. There are people who do not understand. But if we honor our ancestors, then we honor also Yunmen, right? So what is it we honor about Yunmen? Not the killing part, right? Aren't we glad he couldn't do that?
"Today, assuming the abbacy here at Nanming, I have to be forgiving. If I'm not lenient, then people across the great earth will all have to beg for their lives. If the great matter before us cannot be grasped, then I'll go with you all up to the Buddha hall and we'll all take turns giving him a beating! Why? Because if you do not hear the true Way, then the action is not against the rules is not a transgression."

~ Zen's Chinese Heritage by Andy Ferguson ~

DAYI'S "NO MIND"

Dayi Daoxin asked his teacher Jianzhi Sengcan, the Third Ancestor, "What is the mind of the ancient Buddhas?"

Sengcan said, "What kind of mind do you have now?"

Dayi said, "I have no mind."

Sengcan said, "Since you have no mind, why would you think buddhas have mind?"

Dayi immediately ceased to have doubt.

~ Dogen's 300 Koans ~

ANGRY BUDDHA

"A woman who practices reciting Buddha Amitabha's name, is very tough and recites "NAMO AMITABHA BUDDHA" three times daily. Although she is doing this practice for over 10 years, she is still quite mean, shouting at people all the time. She starts her practice lighting incense and hitting a little bell.

 A friend wanted to teach her a lesson, and just as she began her recitation, he came to her door and called out: "Miss Nuyen, Miss Nuyen!".
As this was the time for her practice, she got annoyed, but she said to herself: "I have to struggle against my anger, so I will just ignore it." And she continued: "NAMO AMITABHA BUDDHA, NAMO AMITABHA BUDDHA..."
But the man continued to shout her name, and she became more and more oppressive.
She struggled against it and wondered if she should stop the recitation to give the man a piece of her mind, but she continued reciting: "NAMO AMITABHA BUDDHA, NAMO AMITABHA BUDDHA..."
The man outside heard it and continued: "Miss Nuyen, Miss Nuyen..."

Then she could not stand it anymore, jumped up, slammed the door and went to the gate and shouted: "Why do you have to behave like that? I am doing my practice and you keep on shouting my name over and over!"

The gentleman smiled at her and said: "I just called your name for ten minutes and you are so angry. You have been calling Amitabha Buddha's name for more than ten years now; just imagine how angry he must be by now!"

~"Being Peace" by Thich Nhat Hahn ~

YOU SPIT, I BOW

The morning after Philip Kapleau and Professor Phillips arrived at Ryutakuji Monastery they were given a tour of the place by Abbot Soen Nakagawa. Both Americans had been heavily influenced by tales of ancient Chinese masters who'd destroyed sacred texts, and even images of the Buddha, in order to free themselves from attachment to anything. They were thus surprised and disturbed to find themselves being led into a ceremonial hall, where the Roshi invited them to pay respects to a statue of the temple's founder, Hakuin Zenji, by bowing and offering incense.

On seeing Nakagawa bow before the image, Phillips couldn't contain himself, and burst out: "The old Chinese masters burned or spit on Buddha statues! Why do you bow down before them?"

"If you want to spit, you spit," replied the Roshi. "I prefer to bow."

~ One Bird One Stone: 108 American Zen Stories by Sean Murphy ~

BUDDHAS DO NOT KNOW

Nansen instructed the assembly and said, "All the Buddhas of the three worlds (past, present and future) do not know that there is. The cats and oxen know that there is."

~ Case 69 of Shoyoroku ~

THE BURNING HOUSE

An old, wise man returns from his travels to his large and crumbling mansion to find that it is on fire and his many sons are trapped inside. He tells them the situation and calls on them to come out, but they do not understand what the statement "the house is on fire" means, and they are absorbed with their playthings. So, the father tells them that he has presents outside: goat carts for some, deer carts for others, and bullock carts for the rest. The children then hurry to come out and ask for the carts, but the father does not have them. Instead, he gives each child an enormous and magnificent cart, of a type far beyond any splendor they could have imagined, drawn by white oxen. In modern terms, it is as if the children had expected to receive push-bikes, motor bikes, and automobiles, and each was then presented with a starship. They forget their former expectations and joyfully ride on the marvellous ox carts. The Buddha explains that the father in the story is himself; the house is samsara, which is subject to decay and death and is on fire with the passions; the children are disciples; the promised carts are the various apparent rewards consequent upon following Buddhist teachings and practices; and the ox carts are true liberation.

~ The Lotus Sutra ~

UMMON'S STAFF

Asked by a monk, "What is the doctrine that transcends all Buddhas and Masters?"
Ummon immediately held aloft his staff, and said to the assembled monks, "I call this a staff; what do you call it?"
The monk was silent. Again, Ummon held up the staff, saying "The doctrine transcending all the Buddhas and masters, -was not that what you asked me about?"

~ Mumonkan (Originally titled 'Zen and Zen Classics, Vol. 4'), Translated by R.H. Blyth ~

THE GREAT MEANING

A monk asked Zen Master Qingyuan, "What is the great meaning of the Buddhadharma?"

Qingyuan said, "What is the price of rice in Luling?"

(Master was an eminent disciple of sixth Zen Patriarch Hui-neng. He used to live at Quiet Abode Temple on Mt. Qingyuan, near the old city of Luling [modern Ji'an City in southern Jiangxi Province].)

~ Zen's Chinese Heritage by Andy Ferguson ~

LION CUB AND DONKEY

The National Teacher Nanyang Huizhong entered the hall and said, "Those who study Zen should venerate the words of Buddha. There is but one vehicle for attaining Buddhahood, and that is to understand the great principle that is to connect with the source of mind. If you haven't become clear about the great principle then you haven't embodied the teaching, and you're like a lion cub whose body is still irritated by fleas. And if [in that state] you become a teacher of others, even attaining some worldly renown and fortune, but you are still spreading falsehoods. What good does that do you or anyone else? A skilled axe man does not harm himself with the ax head. What is inside the incense burner can't be carried by a donkey!"

~ Zen's Chinese Heritage by Andy Ferguson ~

CAST OFF THE BUDDHA

A monk asked, "How can one become a Buddha?" The National Teacher Nanyang Huizhong said, "Cast off the Buddha and all beings, and at that moment you'll be liberated."

~ Zen's Chinese Heritage by Andy Ferguson ~

THE PLACE

Someone asked, "What is the place from which all Buddhas come?"
Zen Master Yunmen said, "Next question, please!"

~ Records of Yunmen ~

BEYOND BUDDHA

Zen Master Yunmen mentioned the following episode:

Master Dongshan said: "You must know that there is something which goes beyond 'Buddha.'"
A monk asked, "What is it that goes beyond Buddha?"
Master Dongshan replied: "Non-Buddha."
Master Yunmen commented: "He calls it 'non-' because he can neither name nor attain it!"

~ Records of Yunmen ~

CALLING

Once Zen Master Yunmen said, "I used to say that all sounds are the Buddha's voice, all shapes are the Buddha's form, and that the whole world is the Dharma body. Thus, I quite pointlessly produced views that fit into the category of 'Buddhist teaching.' Right now, when I see a staff, I just call it 'staff,' and when I see a house, I just call it 'house.'"

~ Records of Yunmen ~

DEAD FROGS

Once Zen Master Yunmen said, "What is accomplished when one has mentioned the two words 'Buddha' and 'Dharma'?"
He answered in place of the audience, "Dead frogs!"
(Here frogs stand for people who make a lot of noise yet have little to say.)

~ Records of Yunmen ~

THE NIGHT INTERVIEW OF THE NUN MYOTEI

Myotei was a widow and a woman well known for her strength of character. She trained for some years under Kimon, the 150th Master of Enkakuji temple [in Japan]; on a chance to visit the temple she had an experience while listening to a sermon by him on the Diamond Sutra. In the year 1568, she took part in the Rohatsu training week. [This is the most severe training week of the year; it is at the beginning of
December, when according to tradition the Buddha meditated six days and nights, then looked at the morning star and attained the full realization. There is almost continuous meditation broken only by interviews with the teacher, sutra chanting, meals and tea; this goes on for a week, with very little or no sleep according to the temple. On the morning after the last night's meditation and interviews the participants look together the morning star.]

Before one of the night interviews, she took off her robes and came in without anything at all.
She lay down before the teacher, who picked up the iron nyo-i [ceremonial stick] and thrust it out towards her thighs, saying: 'What trick is this?'
The nun said: 'I present the gate by which all the Buddhas of the three realms come into this world.

The teacher said: 'Unless the Buddhas of the three realms go in, they cannot come out. Let the gate be entered here and now.'
And he sat astride the nun.
She demanded: 'He who should enter, what Buddha is that?'
The teacher said: 'What is to be from the beginning has no "should" about it.'
The nun said: 'He who does not give his name is a barbarian brigand, who is not allowed to enter.'
The teacher said: 'Maitreya Buddha, who was to be born to save people after the death of Shakyamuni Buddha, enters the gate.'
The nun made as if to speak and the teacher quickly cover her mouth. He pressed the iron stick between her thighs, saying: 'Maitreya Buddha enters the gate. Give birth this instant.'
The nun hesitated, and the teacher said: 'This is not true womb; how could this give birth to Maitreya?'
The nun went out, and at the interview the next morning, the teacher said: 'Have you given birth to Maitreya?
The nun cried out with great force: 'He was born quietly last night.'
She caught hold of the teacher and put her hands round the top of his head, saying: 'I invite the Buddha to take the top of this head as the Lion Throne. Let him graciously preach a sermon from it.'
The teacher said: 'The way is one alone, not two, not three.'

The nun said: 'In their abilities, the beings differ in ten thousand ways. How should you stick them to one way?'
The teacher said: 'One general at the head of ten thousand men enters the capital.'

~ Case 52 of The Warrior Kōan ~

WHAT IS NOT BUDDHA DHARMA?

Niaoge Daolin (741-824, also known as Bird's Nest Master) always lives in a bird's nest. He has an attendant named Hui Tung who lives there close to his nest for many years. One day he takes leave from Niao. The latter asks, "Where shall you go?" Hui replies, "I became a monk to learn Buddha dharmas but I did not get any teaching from you. So, I have to seek another teacher."
Niao says, "If you are searching for Buddha dharmas, I also have a little here."
"Where is it?"
Thereupon he takes a tiny feather from the nest, blows it away and asks, "Is this not a Buddha dharma?". Hui Tung instantly comprehends.

~ Source: Unknown ~

YOU MONK TALKATIVE

The Chinese Ch'an master Yao-shan wrote the word "Buddha," and asked Tao-wu Yuan-chih (768-835), one of his successors: "What is that word?"
Tao-wu answered: "It is the word "Buddha".
Yao-shan said: "You monk talkative."
Another monk then asked: "I am not clear, please teach me."
Yao-shan kept silent for a little while then said: "It is not hard for me to tell you some words today, but it would be better if you immediately realize it yourself. If you keep thinking about it, then it will be my fault. This is not as good as if everyone keeps his mouth shut in order to not get involved."

~ Source: Unknown ~

THE BUDDHA

Foguan Ruman (Bukko Nyoman, 752-842?), whose family name was Lu, joined Mazu's monastery in Hongzhou. Later he moved north and eventually took up residence at Jinge monastery on Wutai Mountain. He visited Chang'an in 805 and offered religious instructions to the ailing emperor Shunzong. A record of a conversation between the emperor and Ruman includes this exchange:

Shunzong asked, "Whence did the Buddha come? Where did he go after his passing away? As it is said that he constantly dwells in the world, where is the Buddha right now?"

Ruman said, "The Buddha comes from the unconditioned (wuwei), and after his passing away he goes back to the unconditioned. The dharma body is like empty space - it is constantly present when there is no mind (wuxin). When there is thought, it returns to no-thought (wunian), and where there is abode it returns to no-abode (wuzhu). When coming, he comes for the sake of living beings, and when leaving he leaves for the sake of living beings. The pure ocean of suchness (zhenru) is transparent and its essence abides forever. The wise ones think about it thoughtfully, and then do not give rise to any doubts about it."

~ Ordinary Mind as the Way: The Hongzhou School and the Growth of Chan Buddhism By Mario Poceski ~

THE WORD: BUDDHA

Once Master Zhaozhou addressed the assembly saying, "I don't like to hear the word 'Buddha.'"
A monk came forward and asked, "Then how does the master teach others?"
The master said, "Buddha, Buddha."

~ Treasury of the Forest of Ancestors by Satyavayu of Touching Earth Sangha ~

DONGSHAN'S "GOING BEYOND BUDDHA"

Zen master Dongshan Liangjie [Wuben] of Mount Dong said to the assembly, "Experience going beyond Buddha and say a word."

A monastic asked him, "What is saying a word?"

Dongshan said, "When you say a word, you don't hear it."

The monastic said, "Do you hear it?"

Dongshan said, "When I am not speaking, I hear it."

~ Dogen's 300 Koans ~

HESHAN BEATS THE DRUM

Zen master Wuyan of Heshan [Chengyuan] said in his instruction, "Cultivating study is called learning. Going beyond study is called closeness. To pass beyond these two is called true passing."

A monastic came forward and said, "What is true passing?"

Heshan said, "Heshan knows how to beat the drum."

The monastic said, "What is the true principle?"

Heshan said, "Heshan knows how to beat the drum."

The monastic asked further, "I am not asking you about mind is Buddha. What is no mind, no Buddha?"

Heshan said, "Heshan knows how to beat the drum."

The monastic said, "What is going beyond buddha?"

Heshan said, "Heshan knows how to beat the drum."

~ Dogen's 300 Koans ~

TOUZI ANSWERS "BUDDHA"

A monk asked Touzi Datong, "What is Buddha?"
Touzi answered, "Buddha."
"What is the Way?"
Touzi said, "The Way."
"What is Zen?"
Touzi said, "Zen."

~Entangling Vines: A Classic Collection of Zen Koans by Thomas Yuho Kirchner~

BUDDHA: THE EMPTINESS OF HEART

Zen Master Bukko said:

The way out of life and death is not some special technique; the essential thing is to penetrate to the root of life and death. It is in the center of everyone, and everything else is dependent on it. Zen is to pierce through to it.

Zen sitting is not some sort of operation to be performed. It is going into one's true original nature before father or mother were born. The self seeks to grasp the self, but it is already the self, so why should it go to grasp the self? Look into it. Where was it then? Where is it now? When life ends, where does it go? When you feel you cannot look any more, look and see how that inability to look appears and disappears. As you look and see how the looking arises and goes, satori, realization, will arise of itself.

At the beginning you have to take up a kōan riddle. One such is this: 'What is your true face before father and mother were born'. For one facing the turbulence of life and death, such a kōan clears away the sandy soil and opens up the golden treasure which was there from the beginning, the ageless root of all things.

In concentration on a kōan, there is a time of rousing the spirit of inquiry, a time of breaking clinging attachments, a time of furious dashing forward, and there is a time of damping the fuel and stopping the boiling. In general, meditation has to be done with urgency, but if after three or five years the urgency is still maintained by force, the tension becomes a wrong one and it is a serious condition. Many lose heart and give up. In such a case, the kōan is to be thrown down. Then there is a cooling. The point is that many people come to success if they first have the experience of wrestling with a kōan and later reduce the effort, but few come to success when they are putting out exceptional effort. After a good time, the rush of thoughts outward and inward, subsides naturally, and the true face shows itself as the solution to the kōan. And mind, free from all motivations, always appears as void and absolute sameness, shining like the brightness of heaven, at the center of the vast expanse of phenomenal things, and needing no polishing or cleaning. This is beyond all concepts, beyond being and non-being.

Leave your innumerable knowing and seeings and understandings, and go to that greatness of space. When you come to that vastness, there is no speck of Buddhism in your heart, and then you will have the true sight of the buddhas and patriarchs. The true nature is like the immensity of space, which contains all things. When you can conform to high and low, square and round, to all regions equally, that is it. The emptiness of the sea lets waves rise, the emptiness of the mountain valley makes the voice echo, the emptiness of the heart makes the Buddha. When you empty the heart, things appear as in a mirror, shining there without differences in them: 'Life and death is an illusion, and all the buddhas one's own body'.

~ The Old Zen Master, Translated by Trevor Leggett ~

XUEFENG'S "TURNING THE DHARMA WHEEL"

Zen master Yicun of Mount Xuefeng [Zhenjue] pointed with his finger at a furnace and said to Xuansha, "All buddhas in the three worlds are in here, turning the great dharma wheel."

Xuansha said, "The king's regulations are rather strict."

Xuefeng said, "How so?"

Xuansha said, "Stealing is not permitted."

~ Dogen's 300 Koans ~

DAGUI'S "NO BUDDHA NATURE"

[Guishan] Dagui once said to the assembly, "Sentient beings have no buddha nature."

At another time, Yanguan said to his assembly, "Sentient beings have buddha nature."

Two monastics from Yanguan's community were visiting Dagui to check on his teaching. They heard Dagui's dharma discourse but could not understand the depth of his teaching. They grew arrogant. When they were sitting in the garden, they saw Yangshan coming. They advised him, saying, "Senior brother, it's not easy; you should study Buddhadharma diligently."

Yangshan drew a circle in the air, showed it to them, and threw it over his back. Then he stretched out his arms and asked them to return the circle. The two monastics were dumbfounded and did not know what to do.

Yangshan advised them saying, "It's not easy; you should study the Buddhadharma diligently." He paid his respects and left.

While the two monastics were on their way back to Yanguan, after traveling thirty miles, one of them had realization and said in admiration, "Dagui's words 'Sentient beings have no buddha nature' are not mistaken." He went back to Dagui. The other monastic had realization when he was crossing a river. He said in admiration, "Regarding Dagui's words, 'Sentient beings have no Buddha nature,' there must be a reason for saying that." He also returned to Dagui.

~ Dogen's 300 Koans ~

BUDDHA'S BEGGING BOWL

One day the World-Honored One said to Ānanda, "It is getting close to mealtime. You should go to town with the begging bowl."

Ānanda accepted his request.

The World-Honored One said, "When you go begging with the bowl, you follow the manner of the Past Seven Buddhas."

Ānanda said, "What is the manner of the Past Seven Buddhas?"

The Buddha said, "Ānanda!"

Ānanda responded, "Yes, Master."

The Buddha said, "Go begging."

~ Dogen's 300 Koans ~

FAYAN'S "YOU ARE HUICHAO"

Guizong Cejin [family name Huichao] asked Fayan, "What is Buddha?"

Fayan said, "You are Huichao [literally, 'Going Beyond Wisdom']."

~ Case 252 of Dogen's 300 Koans and Case 7 of The Blue Cliff Record (Hekiganroku)~

THE WORLD-HONORED ONE DID NOT SPEAK A WORD

When the World-Honored One was about to enter parinirvāṇa, Mañjuśrī asked him to give a sermon once more.

The World-Honored One scolded him, saying, "I have not spoken even a word for forty-seven years. You are asking me to speak once more. Have I ever said a word?"

Mañjuśrī was silent.

~ Dogen's 300 Koans ~

THE BUDDHAS

It happened that a Zen seeker came to a Master and asked him, 'I have come from a very long distance, I have travelled thousands of miles to come to your feet.'
The Master asked, 'For what? What do you want?'
The man said, 'I would like to become a Buddha.'
The Master said, 'Get out from here! Already we have too many Buddhas here.'
The Master used to live in a temple which is called 'the Temple of One Thousand and One Buddhas'. There were one thousand and one statues of Buddha.
So he said, 'Get out of it! Immediately out of it. We are tired. We already have one thousand and one Buddhas here, we don't need anyone else. But if you want to become yourself, you can come in.'
Remember, Zen is not an imitation. No Zen Master can ever think of writing a book like Thomas Campus' book 'imitation of Christ'. Impossible. The very title will be laughed at. The real religion is not imitation of anybody else, it is a search to find out your own authentic self, who you are.

~ Dang Dang Doko Dang by Osho ~

THE WOMAN AT THE INN

There was a woman who kept the pilgrim's inn at Hara under Mount Fuji. Her name is unknown, and it is not known when she was born or died.

She went to hear a talk by Hakuin who said, "They say there's a pure land where everything is only mind, and that there's a Buddha of light in your own body. Once that Buddha of light appears, mountains, rivers, earth, grass, trees, and forests suddenly glow with a great light. To see this, you have to look inside your own heart. Then what should you be looking out for? When you are looking for something that is only mind, what kind of special features would it have? When you are looking for the Buddha of infinite light in your own body, how would you recognize it?"

When she heard this, the woman said, "This isn't so hard." Back at home she meditated day and night, holding the question while she was awake and during her sleep. One day, as she was washing a pot, she had a sudden breakthrough. She threw the pot aside and rushed to see Hakuin.

She said, "I've met Buddha in my own body, and everything on earth is shining with a great light! It's wonderful!" She danced for joy.

"Is that so?" said Hakuin, "but what about a pit of shit, does it also shine with a great light?"

The woman ran up and slapped him. She said, "You still don't get it, you old fart!"

Hakuin roared with laughter.

~ Bring me the Rhinoceros by John Tarrant ~

UNDERSTANDING

A great Zen Master, Sozan, was asked to explain the ultimate teaching of the Buddha.

He answered," You won't understand it until you have it."

~ The Path of Love by Osho ~

ESSENCE OF THE BUDDHA'S TEACHING

Someone asked, "What is the essential purport of the Buddha's teaching?"
Mazu said, "It is precisely the point at which you let go of your life."

~ The Records of Mazu and the Making of Classical Chan Literature by Mario Poceski~

NO STUDY

Zen Master Huang-Po once said:

"If you students of the Way wish to become Buddhas, you need study no doctrines whatever, but learn only how to avoid seeking for and attaching yourselves to anything."

~ The Zen Teaching of Huang Po on the Transmission of Mind, Translated by John Blofeld ~

THE WAY

There were two good friends, Chokei and Hofuku. They were talking about the Bodhisattva's way, and Chokei said, "Even if the arhat (an enlightened one) were to have evil desires, still the Tathagata (Buddha) does not have two kinds of words. I say that the Tathagata has words, but no dualistic words."
Hofuku said, "Even though you say so, your comment is not perfect."
Chokei asked, "What is your understanding of the Tathagata's words?"
Hofuku said, "We have had enough discussion, so let's have a cup of tea!"

~ Zen Mind, Beginner's Mind ~
~ Shunryu Suzuki ~

DUMB

Zen Master Joshu entered the hall to address the assembly and said, "Brothers, if for your entire life you do not leave the monastery, and if you do not speak for five or ten years, there is no one who would call you someone who cannot speak. Beyond this, what could even a Buddha do to you? If you do not believe [what I say], you can cut off my head."

~ The Recorded Sayings of Zen Master Joshu, Translated by James Green ~

THE BUDDHA IN THE HOME

One day, a young man named Yang fu left his parents to go to Sichuan (Szechwan) to visit the bodhisattva Wuji.
He met a Zen Master in the way who asked, "Where are you going young man?" "
Yang Fu said, "I am going to study under Wuji the bodhisattva."
"Instead of looking for a mere bodhisattva, you'd be better off looking for the Buddha."
"Do you know where I can find the Buddha?"
"When you return home, a person wearing a blanket and with shoes on the wrong feet will come to greet you. That person is the Buddha."
"Really?"
Yang fu hurried back. Arriving at his home late at night. In her joyful haste to greet her returning son Yang fu's mother three on a blanket and accidentally put her slippers on the wrong feet. Yang fu took one look at her and was suddenly enlightened.

~ Source: Unknown ~

HARD

Eminent monks, it is hard to attain human form and hard to get to hear the Buddha Dharma. If you do not deliver this body in this lifetime, then in what lifetime will you deliver this body? Do all of you people want to study Zen? You must abandon something. Abandon what? Abandon the physical body composed of the four elements [fire, water, earth, and air] and the five clusters [form, sensation, perception, motivational synthesis, consciousness]. Abandon all the karmic consciousness from countless ages past. Investigate what's right under your own feet. Contemplate it, get to the bottom of it. What is the truth of it? Keep investigating and investigating.
Suddenly the mind-flower will send forth light, shining through all the worlds in the ten directions. Then it can be said that "When decisive insight is attained from mind, it responds readily at hand." After that you will be able to transform the earth into gold, and churn the rivers into clarified butter. How could you not be content and happy for life? Do not just occupy yourself with seeking Zen and the Path by reading words in books. The Zen Path is not in books. Even if you read the whole Buddhist canon and the works of all the philosophers, these are all just idle words: when you are facing death, you will not be able to use them at all.

~ Sixin Wuxin ~

FORGETTING SLEEP AND FOOD

Zen Master Yue of Songyuan [1132-1202] studied first as a layman with Hua of Ying-an, but he did not reach accord with him.

He spurred himself on even more, and went to see Jie of Mi-an, who answered whatever he asked. Mi-an sighed and said, "This is only cut and dried Zen."

Yue's efforts became even more intense, to the point that he forgot to sleep or eat. It so happened that Mi-an was in his private room questioning a monk [about the koan], "It is not mind, it is not Buddha, it is not things: what is it?"

Yue, who was standing by his side, was greatly enlightened.

~ Meditating with Koans by Zhuhong, Translated by J C Cleary ~

THE TATHĀGATA

"Subhūti, what do you think, can the Tathāgata be seen by his physical marks?
"No, World Honored One, the Tathāgata cannot be seen by his physical marks and why? It is because the physical marks are spoken of by the Tathāgata as no physical marks."
The Buddha said to Subhūti, "All with marks is empty and false. If you can see all marks as no marks, then you see the Tathāgata."

~ The Diamond Sutra, Chapter 5 ~

NOTHING ATTAINED, NOTHING SPOKEN

"Subhūti, what do you think? Has the Tathāgata attained Anuttara-samyakasambodhi (Unparalleled Perfect Enlightenment)? Has the Tathāgata spoken any Dharma?"
Subhūti said, "As I understand what the Buddha has said, there is no concrete dharma called Anuttara-samyakasambodhi, and there is no concrete dharma which the Tathāgata has spoken. And why? The dharmas spoken by the Tathāgata cannot be grasped and cannot be spoken. They are neither dharmas nor no dharmas. And why? Unconditioned dharmas distinguish worthy sages."

~ The Diamond Sutra, Chapter 7 ~

NOTHING SPOKEN

"Subhūti, what do you think? Is there any Dharma spoken by the Tathāgata?"
Subhūti said to the Buddha. "No, World Honored One, nothing has been spoken by the Tathāgata."
||Ch. 13||
Buddha said to Subhūti, "Subhūti, do not say the Tathāgata has the thought, 'I have spoken dharma.' Do not think that way. And why? If someone says the Tathāgata has spoken dharma, he slanders the Buddha due to his inability to understand what I say." ||Ch. 21||

~ The Diamond Sutra, Chapter 13, 21 ~

AND THE FLOWERS SHOWERED

Subhūti was one of Buddha's disciple. He was able to understand the potency of emptiness, the viewpoint that nothing exists except in its relationship of subjectivity and objectivity.

One day Subhūti, in a mood of sublime emptiness, was sitting under a tree. Flowers began to fall about him.

"We are praising you for your discourse on emptiness," the gods whispered to him.

"But I have not spoken of emptiness," said Subhūti.

"You have not spoken of emptiness, we have not heard emptiness," responded the gods. "This is the true emptiness." And blossoms showered upon Subhūti as rain.

~ Zen Flesh, Zen Bones by Nyogen Senzaki and Paul Reps ~

VERBAL TEACHINGS

The verbal teachings of Buddhas and Zen masters that have come down from the past are like bits of tile used to knock on a door; it is a matter of expediency that we use them as entrances into truth.
For some years now, students have not been getting to the root of the aim of Zen, instead taking the verbal teachings of Buddhas and Zen masters to the ultimate rule. That is like ignoring a hundred thousand pure clear oceans and only focusing attention on a single bubble.

~ Ying-an ~
~ The Zen Reader, by Thomas Cleary ~

LOOKING FOR BUDDHAS

There is no real doctrine at all for you to chew on or squat over. If you will not believe in yourself, you pick up your baggage and go around to other people's houses, looking for Zen, looking for Tao, looking for mysteries, looking for marvels, looking for Buddhas, looking for Zen masters, looking for teachers.
You think this is searching for the ultimate, and you make it into your religion, but this is like running blindly to the east to get something that is in the west. The more you run, the further away you are, and the more you hurry the later you become. You just tire yourself, to what benefit in the end?

~ Yuansou ~
~ The Zen Reader, by Thomas Cleary ~

THE WAY OF BUDDHAS AND ZEN MASTERS

The Way of Buddhas and Zen masters is open as cosmic space, vast as the ocean – how can careless mediocrities tell of it? And how can it be measured like feet and inches, or calculated like thatch? Only those of great faculties, great apacity, and great power, exerting great intensity, stomp right through where not a single thought has arisen, not a single bubble has emerged, after that sitting and reclining on the heads of the Buddhas and Zen masters. Only then do they have a little bit of realization.

~ Hsueh-yen ~
~ The Zen Reader, by Thomas Cleary ~

NOT SEEKING

A Buddha is one who does not seek. In seeking this, you turn away from it. The principle is the principle of non-seeking; when you see it, you lose it.
If you cling to non-seeking, this is the same as seeking. If you cling to non-striving, this is the same as striving.
Thus, the Diamond Cutter Scripture says, "Do not grasp truth, do not grasp untruth, and do not grasp that which is not untrue."
It also says, "The truth that the Buddhas find has no reality or unreality."

~ Zen Master Baizhang Huaihai (720-814) ~
~ The Zen Reader, by Thomas Cleary ~

PITY

It is a pity that deluded people do not understand; they arbitrarily cling to doctrines and turn them into sicknesses, using sickness to attack sickness. They make it so they get further estranged from Buddha nature the more they seek it. The more they hurry, the more they're delayed.

~ Kao-feng ~
~ The Zen Reader, by Thomas Cleary ~

BUDDHA

What is disturbing you and making you uneasy is that there are things outside and mind inside. Therefore, even when the ordinary and the holy are one reality, there still remains a barrier of view. So it is said that as long as views remain you are ordinary; when feelings are forgotten you're a buddha. I advise you, don't seek reality, just stop views.

~ Fa-yen ~
~ The Zen Reader, by Thomas Cleary ~

THE PURE LIGHT

There is no stability in the world; it is like a house on fire. This is not a place where you can stay for a long time. The murderous demon of impermanence is instantaneous, and it does not choose between the upper and lower classes, or between the old and the young.
If you want to be no different from the Buddhas and Zen masters, just don't seek externally.
The pure light in a moment of awareness in your mind is the Buddha's essence within you. The non-discriminating light in a moment of awareness in your mind is the Buddha's wisdom within you. The undifferentiated light in a moment of awareness in your mind is the Buddha's manifestation within you.

~ Zen Master Rinzai ~
~ The Zen Reader, by Thomas Cleary ~

EVERYWHERE

Ta-sui was asked, "Buddha's truth is everywhere; so, where do you teach students to plant their feet?"
He replied, "The vast ocean lets fish leap freely; the endless sky lets birds fly freely."

~ The Zen Reader, by Thomas Cleary ~

SAME OR DIFFERENT?

Zen Master Haryō Kōkan was once asked by one of his monks, "Are the intent of our Ancestor Bodhidharma and the intent of the Teachings of Buddha the same or are they different?"
The Master replied, "When a hen is cold, it perches in a tree; when a duck is cold, it enters the water."

~ Shobogenzo by Zen Master Dogen ~

SAME OR DIFFERENT?

Someone asked Zen Master Mu-chou Tao-tsung: "Are the teachings of Buddha and the teachings of the Patriarch [Bodhidharma] the same?"
The master replied: "A green mountain is a green mountain, and white clouds are white clouds."

~ The Original Teachings of Ch'an Buddhism by Chang Ching Yuan ~

THE SOURCE

A monk asked, "What is that direct approach to the Source to which Buddha would give his seal of approval?"

At this, the Zen Master Hsiang-yen Chih-hsien threw away his staff and walked out with his hands empty.

~ The Original Teachings of Ch'an Buddhism by Chang Ching Yuan ~

BUDDHA

Someone asked, "What is Buddha?"
Zen Master Joshu said, "Are you Buddha?"

~ Radical Zen by Yoel Hoffman ~

YUANWU'S "GATE OF MISFORTUNE"

A monk asked Yuanwu Keqin, "What is Buddha?" Yuanwu replied, "The mouth is the gate of misfortune."

~ Entangling Vines: A Classic Collection of Zen Koans by Thomas Yuho Kirchner~

SECRET

A little story about a Zen Master:
A disciple asked the Master," What is Buddha's truth?"
The Master said," Why not ask about your own mind or self instead of somebody else's?"
" What then is my self, O Master?" asked the disciple.
" You have to see what is known as 'the secret act.'"
" What is 'the secret act'? Tell me, Master," asked the disciple.
The Master opened his eyes and closed them.
This is the secret act.

~ Ecstasy, The Forgotten Language by Osho ~

THE FUNDAMENTAL TEACHING

Monk: "What is the fundamental idea of Buddhism?"
Yun-men: "When spring comes, the grass turns green of itself."

~ Records of Yunmen ~

STRIKING THE BUDDHA

When Zen Master Taego (1301-1382) was appointed as the abbot of Bongeun Seon monastery, he occupied the room of the abbot, picked up his staff and put it down once, saying, "If a Buddha comes here, I will strike him, and if a patriarch comes I will strike him."

He pointed at the Dharma-throne and said, "The innumerable Buddhas and patriarchs have shat here, filing the heavens with a stink and filing up the entire sahā (endurance of suffering) world. Today I cannot avoid pouring the waters of the four great oceans (over it) to wash and make it neat and clean. Great assembly, do not say it is even messier."

~ (Collected Works of Korean Buddhism, Volume 8) Seon Dialogues, Edited and Translated by John Jorgensen ~

HEEDFULNESS

Buddha said, "The fires of impermanence burn up all the worlds." He also said, "The fires of suffering of sentient beings burn all round." He also said, "The bandits of the frustrations are always looking (for opportunities) to kill people." Persons of the Way should appropriately warn themselves, like trying to save their head if it is on fire.
I respectfully inform persons investigating the profound, do not pass time in vain.

~ Seonga Gwigam ~
~ The Great Master Seosan Hyujeong (1520-1604) ~
~ (Collected Works of Korean Buddhism, Volume 3) Hyujeong, Selected Works Edited and Translated by John Jorgensen ~

UNDERSTANDING OF BUDDHA

A monk asked, "If someone is seeking an understanding of Buddha, what's the best path to doing so?"
Zen Master Fayan Wenyi (885-958) said, "It doesn't pass here."

~ Zen's Chinese Heritage by Andy Ferguson ~

THE ULTIMATE TEACHING

A monk asked, "What is the ultimate teaching of all Buddhas?"

Zen Master Fayan Wenyi (885-958) said, "You have it too."

~ Zen's Chinese Heritage by Andy Ferguson ~

WHO IS THAT PERSON?

Yung-a Chuan-teng said to his assembly, "There is a certain person, who avers, 'I do not depend on the blessing and help of the Buddha, I do not live in any of the three realms, I do not belong to the world of the five elements. The Patriarchs have not dared to pin me down, nor have the Buddha dared to give me a definite name.' Can you tell me who is that Person?"

Wu-hsieh Ling-meh, a disciple of Shih-t'ou as well as of Ma-tsu, was once asked by a monk, "What is greater than the heaven-and-earth?"

He replied, "No man can know him!"

~ The Golden Age of Zen ~

ZEN

Emperor Go-Uta asked Shinchi Kakushin about Zen. Kakushin told him: "A Buddha is one who understands mind. The ordinary fellow does not understand mind. You cannot achieve this by depending upon others. To attain Buddhahood, you must look into your own mind."

~ Zen Masters of Japan by Richard Bryan McDaniel ~

WHAT IS BUDDHA?

The monk Lingxun of Furong Shan, on his first visit to Zen Master Guizong Zhichang, asked, "What is Buddha?"

"Would you believe it if I told you?" replied the master.

"If the venerable sir would express it sincerely and truthfully, how could one presume not to believe it?" said the monk.

"It is just you," said the master.

~ Records of the Transmission of the Lamp (Jingde Chuandeng Lu) by Daoyuan, translated by Randolph S Whitfield ~

THE BUDDHA-NATURE

A monk asked the Venerable Yingtian of Yizhou, "Every person has the Buddha-nature - what is the venerable's Buddha-nature?"

"What do you call the Buddha-nature?" answered the master.

"Put like this, the venerable sir does not have the Buddha-nature," said the monk.

"Just so! Just so!" exclaimed the master.

~ Records of the Transmission of the Lamp (Jingde Chuandeng Lu) by Daoyuan, translated by Randolph S Whitfield ~

TONGUE

A monk asked, "What is Buddha?"
Zen Master Lingguan of Wushi Shan Monastery showed his tongue and the monk bowed.
"Stop! Stop! What have you seen to bow like that?"
"Thanks to the venerable sir's compassion for showing his tongue," replied the monk.
"The day is approaching when a boil will arise on the old chap's tongue," replied the master.

~ Records of the Transmission of the Lamp (Jingde Chuandeng Lu) by Daoyuan, translated by Randolph S Whitfield ~

THE BUDDHA

A monk asked, 'What is Buddha?'
'A question,' replied Zen Master Shouqing of Mount Qingquan.
'What about the patriarchs?'
'Answer.'

~ Records of the Transmission of the Lamp (Jingde Chuandeng Lu) by Daoyuan, translated by Randolph S Whitfield ~

THE PRINCIPAL THRUST

A monk asked Zen Master Hengzhou Guangfan, 'What is the principal thrust of the Buddha-dharma?'
'Verification,' replied the master

~ Records of the Transmission of the Lamp (Jingde Chuandeng Lu) by Daoyuan, translated by Randolph S Whitfield ~

THE BUDDHAS

A monk asked, 'What is the source of all the Buddhas?'
Zen Master Xiufu Wukong replied, 'What do you mean by all the Buddhas?'

~ Records of the Transmission of the Lamp (Jingde Chuandeng Lu) by Daoyuan, translated by Randolph S Whitfield ~

THE BUDDHA-DHARMA

'What is the Buddha-dharma?'
'Great corruption,' replied the Zen master Shaoxiu.

~ Records of the Transmission of the Lamp (Jingde Chuandeng Lu) by Daoyuan, translated by Randolph S Whitfield ~

THE BUDDHA

A monk asked, 'What is Buddha?'
Zen Master Daoquan (930-985 CE) replied, 'After the snows have departed, the spring arrives quite naturally.'

~ Records of the Transmission of the Lamp (Jingde Chuandeng Lu) by Daoyuan, translated by Randolph S Whitfield ~

THE MAIN PURPORT

A monk asked Zen master Jingru, the second-generation incumbent of Mount Dalong [Zhejiang, Changde], 'What is the main purport of the Buddha-dharma?'
The master shouted.
'What is your reverence's meaning?' asked the monk.
'Understood?' replied the master.
'Not understood.'
The master gave another shout.

~ Records of the Transmission of the Lamp (Jingde Chuandeng Lu) by Daoyuan, translated by Randolph S Whitfield~

THE MIND OF ANCIENT BUDDHAS

A monk asked, 'What is the mind of the ancient Buddhas like?'
Zen Master Tiantai Deshao replied, 'This is not a bad question.'

~ Records of the Transmission of the Lamp (Jingde Chuandeng Lu) by Daoyuan, translated by Randolph S Whitfield ~

THE MAIN THRUST

A monk asked, 'What is the main thrust of the Buddha-dharma?'
Zen Master Daguan Zhiyun (906-969 CE) replied, 'Exactly the right question.'
'Then the student can make prostrations.'
'What have you understood?' asked the master.

~ Records of the Transmission of the Lamp (Jingde Chuandeng Lu) by Daoyuan, translated by Randolph S Whitfield ~

THE MEANING

A monk asked the Zen Master Fadeng Taiqin (910-974 CE), 'What is the cardinal meaning of the Buddha-dharma?'
'First ask about the lesser meaning, then you will get the big meaning,' answered the master.

~ Records of the Transmission of the Lamp (Jingde Chuandeng Lu) by Daoyuan, translated by Randolph S Whitfield ~

THE QUESTION

A monk asked Zen Master Fa'an Huiji, 'What is the mind of the ancient Buddhas like?'
'What an expectant question!' said the master.

~ Records of the Transmission of the Lamp (Jingde Chuandeng Lu) by Daoyuan, translated by Randolph S Whitfield ~

HOW MANY TIMES?

A monk asked Zen Master Dazhi Daochang (916-991 CE), 'What is Buddha?'
'How many times have you not asked?'

~ Records of the Transmission of the Lamp (Jingde Chuandeng Lu) by Daoyuan, translated by Randolph S Whitfield ~

THE BUDDHA

A monk asked, 'What is Buddha?'
'Were I to tell you, it would be something apart,'
said the Zen master Fashi Cezhen (905-979 CE).

~ Records of the Transmission of the Lamp (Jingde Chuandeng Lu) by Daoyuan, translated by Randolph S Whitfield ~

THE POINTER

A monk asked Master Guxian Jin, 'What is Buddha?'
'Point to yourself,' said the master.

~ Records of the Transmission of the Lamp (Jingde Chuandeng Lu) by Daoyuan, translated by Randolph S Whitfield ~

WHO TO ASK?

A monk asked Zen Master Shanglan Shouna, 'What is Buddha?'
'Who to ask?' replied the master.

~ Records of the Transmission of the Lamp (Jingde Chuandeng Lu) by Daoyuan, translated by Randolph S Whitfield ~

NOT KNOWN

A monk asked Ven. Fuzhou Fuchan, 'What is Buddha?'
'Not known,' said the master.

~ Records of the Transmission of the Lamp (Jingde Chuandeng Lu) by Daoyuan, translated by Randolph S Whitfield ~

CRAZY FELLOW

A monk asked Zen Master Gaoli Lingjian, 'What is Buddha?'
'Throw this crazy fellow out!' said the master.

~ Records of the Transmission of the Lamp (Jingde Chuandeng Lu) by Daoyuan, translated by Randolph S Whitfield ~

WHAT IS NOT?

A monk asked Zen Master Huicheng (941-1007 CE), 'What is Buddha?'
'What is not?' replied the master.

~ Records of the Transmission of the Lamp (Jingde Chuandeng Lu) by Daoyuan, translated by Randolph S Whitfield ~

THE MEANING

A monk asked, 'What is the deep meaning of the Buddha's Dharma?'
Zen master Magu Baoche maintained silence.

~ Records of the Transmission of the Lamp (Jingde Chuandeng Lu) by Daoyuan, translated by Randolph S Whitfield ~

THE BUDDHA

A monk asked, 'What is Buddha?'
'A cat atop the naked pillar,' said the Zen master Pishu Huixing.
'The student does not understand,' said the monk.
'Then go and ask the naked pillar,' answered the master.

~ Records of the Transmission of the Lamp (Jingde Chuandeng Lu) by Daoyuan, translated by Randolph S Whitfield ~

EVADING

A monk asked Zen Master Yuezhou Qianfeng, 'What is the talk beyond Buddha, beyond the patriarchs?'
'The old monk is asking you,' replied the master.
'The venerable sir is evading.'
'The old monk's question came from not understanding; the question is what the talk beyond Buddha, beyond patriarchs is!' replied the master.

~ Records of the Transmission of the Lamp (Jingde Chuandeng Lu) by Daoyuan, translated by Randolph S Whitfield ~

DEATH POEMS

DOYU
(*Died on the fifth day of the second month, 1256* at the age of fifty-six)
In all my six and fifty years
No miracles occurred.
For the Buddhas and the Great Ones of the Faith,
I have questions in my heart.
And if I say,
"Today, this hour
I leave the world,"
There's nothing in it. Day after day,
Does not the sun rise in the east?

ZOSO ROYO
(Died on the fifth day of the sixth month, 1276 at the age of eighty-four)

I pondered Buddha's teaching
A full four and eighty years.
The gates are all now locked about me.
No one was ever here—
Who then is he about to die,
And why lament for nothing?
Farewell!
The night is clear,
The moon shines calmly,
The wind in the pines
Is like a lyre's song.
With no I and no other
Who hears the sound?

ENSETSU
(Died on the nineteenth day of the ninth month, 1743 at the age of seventy-three)

Autumn gust:
I have no further business
in this world.

Ensetsu grew up in a Zen Buddhist temple and in his later years served as a priest. To the haiku written before his death he attached, as was the custom among Zen monks, a death poem in Chinese as well:

Many things befell me as I followed Buddha
Three and seventy years.
What is death?
Freely, from my own true self,
Ho! Ho!

"Ho!" is a translation of totsu, a cry of enlightenment.

Ensetsu was very much attached to his haiku master, Rosen, with whom he roamed all over Japan. When Ensetsu heard of his master's having fallen ill, he hastened to his side, though he himself was suffering from severe stomach pains. From the day Rosen died, Ensetsu's disease worsened, and he survived his master less than a month.

~ Japanese Death Poems by Yoel Hoffmann ~

THE STICK

GOKU KYONEN
(*Died on the eighth day of the tenth month, 1272 at the age of fifty-six*)

The truth embodied in the Buddhas
   Of the future, present, past;
The teaching we received from the
   Fathers of our faith
Can all be found at the tip of my stick.

When Goku felt his death was near, he ordered all his monk-disciples to gather around him. He sat at the pulpit, raised his stick, gave the floor a single tap with it, and said the poem above. When he finished, he raised the stick again, tapped the floor once more and cried, "See! See!" Then, sitting upright, he died.

~ Japanese Death Poems by Yoel Hoffmann ~

KILL THE BUDDHA

Shumpo Soki
(Died on the fourteenth day of the first month, 1496
at the age of eighty-eight)

My sword leans against the sky.
With its polished blade I'll behead
The Buddha and all of his saints.
Let the lightning strike where it will.

It is said that after reciting this poem, Shumpo gave a single "laugh of derision" and died. To "behead The Buddha" suggests spiritual independence and an awareness freed from the manner of thought dictated by religious tradition. According to Buddhist belief, a man who sins against religion and morality is liable to die by a stroke of lightning.

~ Japanese Death Poems by Yoel Hoffmann ~

THE BUDDHA

A monk asked Chan master Panlong Kewen, 'What is Buddha?'
'A foolish child rejecting father and absconding,' said the master.

~ Records of the Transmission of the Lamp (Jingde Chuandeng Lu) by Daoyuan, translated by Randolph S Whitfield ~

THE SOURCE

A monk asked Zen Master Zhiyong, 'What is the original source of all the Buddhas?'
'What is the source of this question?', replied the master.

~ Records of the Transmission of the Lamp (Jingde Chuandeng Lu) by Daoyuan, translated by Randolph S Whitfield ~

THE BUDDHA

Question: 'What is Buddha?'
'Mistake,' replied the master Tianwang Yuan.

~ Records of the Transmission of the Lamp (Jingde Chuandeng Lu) by Daoyuan, translated by Randolph S Whitfield ~

OBSCURE AND DISTANT

Zen Master Sixin Wuxin (1044-1115) entered the hall and addressed the monks, saying, "It's deep, obscure, distant, and no person can go there. Did Shakyamuni go there or not? If he went there, why can't anyone else? If he didn't go there, who says it's obscure and distant?"

~ Zen's Chinese Heritage by Andy Ferguson ~

PRACTICE

[Many times, Zen Masters are known by the name of the mountain where their monastery was located.]

Zen Master Yangqi addressed the monks, saying, "There is no great meaning on Yangqi. What you sow you'll reap! Old Shakyamuni was talking in a dream. Where will you find any trace of it now?"

Yangqi then struck the meditation platform and shouted, "Practice!"

~ Zen's Chinese Heritage by Andy Ferguson ~

NOTHING ATTAINED

Subhūti said to the Buddha, "World Honored One, is it that the Tathāgata in attaining Anuttara-samyakasambodhi (unparalleled perfect enlightenment) did not attain anything?"
The Buddha said, "So it is, so it is, Subhūti. As to Anuttara-samyakasambodhi, there is not even the slightest dharma which I could attain, therefore it is called Anuttara-samyakasambodhi."

~ The Diamond Sutra, Chapter 22 ~

BIBLIOGRAPHY

1. The Zen Teaching of Bodhidharma, Translated by Red Pine
2. The Record of Rinzai
3. Zen's Chinese Heritage by Andy Ferguson
4. Records of the Transmission of the Lamp (Jingde Chuandeng Lu, Vol 1-6) by Daoyuan, translated by Randolph S. Whitfield
5. Treasury of the Forest of Ancestors by Satyavayu
6. Zen Flesh, Zen Bones by Nyogen Senzaki and Paul Reps
7. Radical Zen (Recorded Sayings of Joshu) by Yoel Hoffman
8. The Recorded Sayings of Zen Master Joshu, Translated by James Green
9. Talking about Food Doesn't Appease Hunger: Phrases on hunger in Chan (Zen) Buddhist texts by Anu Niemi
10. Hekiganroku (The Blue Cliff Record)
11. Shoyoroku
12. Mumonkan
13. Mumonkan (Originally titled 'Zen and Zen Classics, Vol. 4'), Translated by R.H. Blyth
14. Dogen's 300 Koans
15. Shobogenzo by Dogen
16. Zen Koans by Venerable Gyomay M. Kubose

17. Zen Speaks: Shouts of Nothingness by Tsai Chih Chung
18. The Original Teachings of Ch'an Buddhism by Chang Ching Yuan
19. The Golden Age of Zen: Zen Masters of the T'ang by John Ching Hsiung Wu
20. Zen, The Path of Paradox, Vol 3 by Osho
21. A Bird on the Wing by Osho
22. Entangling Vines: A Classic Collection of Zen Koans by Thomas Yuho Kirchner
23. Sun-Face Buddha: The Teachings of Ma-tsu and the Hung-chou School of Ch'an; Introduced and Translated by Cheng Chien Bhikshu
24. The Records of Mazu and the Making of Classical Chan Literature by Mario Poceski
25. (Collected Works of Korean Buddhism, Volume 3) Hyujeong, Selected Works Edited and Translated by John Jorgensen
26. (Collected Works of Korean Buddhism, Volume 7-1) Gongan Collections I Edited and Translated by John Jorgensen
27. (Collected Works of Korean Buddhism, Volume 7-2) Gongan Collections II Edited and Translated by John Jorgensen
28. (Collected Works of Korean Buddhism, Volume 8) Seon Dialogues, Edited and Translated by John Jorgensen
29. Being Peace by Thich Nhat Hahn

30. One Bird One Stone: 108 American Zen Stories by Sean Murphy
31. Records of Yunmen (Master Yunmen, From the Record of the Chan Teacher "Gate of the Clouds" published by Kodansha International)
32. The Warrior Koans
33. The Old Zen Master, Translated by Trevor Leggett
34. Take It Easy, Vol 1, by Osho
35. Dang Dang Doko Dang by Osho
36. The Path of Love by Osho
37. The Buddha, The Emptiness Of The Heart by Osho
38. Zen: The Mystery and The Poetry of The Beyond by Osho
39. A Sudden Clash of Thunder by Osho
40. Meditating with Koans by Zhuhong, Translated by J. C. Cleary
41. The Zen Reader by Thomas Cleary
42. Ecstasy, The Forgotten Language by Osho
43. Kyozan, A True Man of Zen by Osho
44. Zen: The Quantum Leap from Mind to No Mind by Osho
45. Zen Masters of China by Richard Bryan McDaniel
46. Zen Masters of Japan by Richard Bryan McDaniel
47. Japanese Death Poems by Yoel Hoffman

48. The Iron Flute: 100 Zen Koans by Nyogen Senzaki, Ruth Strout-McCandless
49. The Zen Doctrine of No-Mind by D. T. Suzuki
50. Zen and Zen Classics, Vol 3, by R.H. Blyth
51. Every End Exposed: The 100 Koans of Master Kido - With the Answers of Hakuin - Zen
52. Alagaddupama Sutta
53. The Lotus Sutra
54. Record of the life of the Ch'an master Po-chang Huai-hai [Bojang Whyhigh] Translated by Gary Snyder
55. Ordinary Mind as the Way: The Hongzhou School and the Growth of Chan Buddhism By Mario Poceski
56. The Zen Teaching of Huang Po on the Transmission of Mind, Translated by John Blofeld
57. Zen Mind, Beginner's Mind by Shunryu Suzuki
58. Bring me the Rhinoceros by John Tarrant
59. Teaching Letters of Zen Master Seung Sahn
60. Web Resources:
   - http://www.sinc.sunysb.edu/Clubs/buddhism/story/story.html
   - Zen Humor: Classic Humor from the Zen - Chan - Son Buddhist Tradition by Timothy Conway

https://www.enlightened-spirituality.org/Zen_Humor.html
- Poetry China http://poetrychina.net/Story_of_Zen/zenstory13.htm

www.ingramcontent.com/pod-product-compliance
Lightning Source LLC
Chambersburg PA
CBHW051938290426
44110CB00015B/2031